MIFFLIN
LEWI:

Presented by

PAUL S. LEHMAN

In Memory of

HAROLD D. COHEN

Hollywood Greats of the Golden Years

Hollywood Greats
of the Golden Years
*The Late Stars of the
1920s through the 1950s*

J.G. ELLROD

McFarland & Company, Inc., Publishers
Jefferson, North Carolina, and London

0 ᴬᵀ

British Library cataloguing-in-publication data are available

Library of Congress Cataloguing-in-Publication Data

Ellrod, J.G., 1924–
    Hollywood greats of the golden years : the late stars of the 1920s
through the 1950s / by J.G. Ellrod.
        p.   cm.
    Includes index.
    ISBN 0-89950-371-3 (lib. bdg. : 50# alk. paper) ∞
    1. Motion picture actors and actresses--United States—Biography—
Dictionaries. 2. Motion picture actors and actresses—California—
Los Angeles—Biography—Dictionaries. 3. Hollywood (Los Angeles,
Calif.)—Biography—Dictionaries. I. Title.
PN1998.2.E45   1989
791.43′028′092273—dc20
    [B]   89-42713
                                                                                               CIP

©1989 J.G. Ellrod. All rights reserved

Printed in the United States of America

McFarland & Company, Inc., Publishers
  Box 611, Jefferson, North Carolina 28640

141740

Table of Contents

Introduction

As a child living in Champaign-Urbana, Illinois, I was introduced to the movies via the Western and the weekly serial. Each Saturday afternoon at two I went faithfully to the movie theatre to see one of my favorite cowboy heroes and the next chapter of the current serial. The serial ran about twenty minutes and left the hero or heroine in some deadly danger each week for at least twelve episodes. During the week my friends and I would discuss the serial and how the characters could be saved.

One eventful day the Rialto, a first-run theatre, was showing a movie starring a new personality about whom everyone was talking. So instead of seeing my usual Western and serial, I went to the Rialto. The new personality was Mae West and she was appearing in *She Done Him Wrong*. This film opened another door for me, revealing another world of fantasy and illusion at the movies. The coming attraction preview fascinated me (as had Mae West) even more than the Westerns and the serials. I decided that the next Saturday I would spend my ten cents (child's admission) at the Rialto or RKO Virginia instead of my usual five cents for the Western and the serial at the Park.

After my family moved to Chicago came vaudeville, orchestras, and musicals. I was immersed in the joys of the theatre. I got a job changing the signs which posted the current and coming attractions at our two neighborhood theatres—the Dearborn and the Windsor. I earned twenty-five cents an hour and could watch all the movies for free.

I had one disappointment during this exciting time. One week at the RKO Palace they advertised Ginger Rogers and George Brent *In Person*. I read the advertisement too quickly. This theatre had vaudeville, but they also showed one film with the vaudeville. I wasn't the only person who misread the newspaper. *In Person,* turned out to be the name of the *movie* showing that week. Despite this disappointment, I was ensnared by the glamour and glory of Hollywood.

The stars selected for this book personified the Golden Age of Hollywood when that town was America's dream capital and its inhabitants were America's royalty. The glamour which surrounded the film industry has long since faded and will probably not come again but these stars will live on in the hearts and memories of people everywhere.

A star is defined by Webster's as (1)"a highly publicized theatrical or motion picture performer"; this is obviously so in regard to the present book. But the dictionary also gives (2) "an outstandingly talented performer"; this is not necessarily true of the persons herein.

There have been numerous stars with no discernible dramatic talent. On the other hand, there have been many very talented performers who never became stars. The actors and actresses chosen for this book became stars because they had that certain something— unmistakeable if indefinable—the public clamors for. The stars and their roles showed us life itself during the Golden Age from the late 1920s to the mid–'50s. It was around then that television began to be the main medium of entertainment. Not coincidentally, the studio system began to fall apart in the mid–'50s, with strikes, trade disputes, antitrust actions, witch hunts, and the flight of potential movie audiences to the suburbs. The ever improving television programs meanwhile continued to have the additional advantage of being free.

This book does not attempt to cover all the stars or fine supporting actors and actresses of this Golden Age. What it does hope to do is to bring back into our common memories some of the stars and movies of the past and perhaps stir the reader to research these and other performers of a very important period in film history. The Hollywood stars in this book are some of the brightest, the most loved and the most enduring; the one strict criterion observed in their selection was that they were no longer alive as of 1989. Still, the memory lingers on.

Reference Works Consulted

New York Times Directory of the Film. New York: Arno/Random House, 1971.
Variety Film Reviews Volumes 3–16. New York: Garland, 1983.
Obituary notices from the following newspapers: *Miami Herald, New Orleans Times-Picayune, New York Times, Variety.*

Abbreviation Key

AA   Allied Artists
AFT   American Film Theatre
AIP   American International
Pictures
BIP   British International
Pictures
BV   Buena Vista
Col.   Columbia Pictures
DCA   Distributing Corporation
of America
EL   Eagle Lion Classics
Fox   Fox Picture Corporation
GB   Gaumont-British Studios
GN   Grand National Pictures
Ind.   Independent Release
Lip.   Lippert Pictures
MGM   Metro-Goldwyn-Mayer,
Inc.

Mon.   Monogram Pictures
NGP   National General Pictures
Par.   Paramount Pictures
PRC   Producers Releasing Cor-
poration
PRO   Producers Releasing
Organization
Rank   J. Arthur Rank
Rep.   Republic Pictures
RKO   RKO Radio Pictures
Tif.   Tiffany
20th   20th Century–Fox Film
Corporation
UA   United Artists
Univ.   Universal Pictures,
Universal-International
WB   Warner Brothers Pictures
and First National Pictures

Hollywood Greats
of the Golden Years

George Arliss
(1868–1946)

After working for his father, who was a publisher, Arliss began his theatrical career at the age of eighteen and toured the provinces. He married Florence Montgomery, an actress, in 1899. They appeared together in many plays before coming to America in 1902 in *The Second Mrs. Tangueray* with Mrs. Patrick Campbell. On Broadway he supported Blanche Bates and Mrs. Fiske. He reached stardom in *The Devil* by Molnar.

He recreated many of his stage successes in silent films. A sound version of *Disraeli* won him an Academy Award in 1929–30. He returned to Broadway in 1929 as Shylock in *The Merchant of Venice*. He wrote two autobiographies, *Up the Years from Bloomsbury,* 1927, and *My Ten Years at the Studios,* 1940. He retired from the screen in 1937.

George Arliss Sound Film Credits (1929–1937)

Disraeli (WB, 1929)
The Green Goddess (WB, 1930)
Old English (WB, 1930)
Millionaire (WB, 1931)
Alexander Hamilton (WB, 1931)
The Man Who Played God (WB, 1932)
Successful Calamity (WB, 1932)
King's Vacation (WB, 1933),
Working Man (WB, 1933)
Voltaire (WB, 1933)
House of Rothschild (UA, 1934)
Last Gentleman (UA, 1934)

1

Top: George Arliss as Rothschild offers Boris Karloff, the Prussian ambassador, money to defeat Napoleon in *The House of Rothschild* (United Artists, 1934). *Bottom:* Ralph Forbes, H.B. Warner and Alice Joyce have survived a plane crash and find themselves prisoners of an English-hating Rajah played by George Arliss in *The Green Goddess* (Warner Bros., 1930).

Cardinal Richelieu (UA, 1935)
Iron Duke (GB, 1935)
The Guv'nor (Mister Hobo — GB, 1935)

East Meets West (GB, 1936)
Man of Affairs (GB, 1937)
Dr. Syn (GB, 1937).

Fred Astaire
(1899–1987)

Fred Astaire was born in Omaha, Nebraska. He and his sister, Adele, were taken to New York for professional dance training in 1906 by their mother. They toured in vaudeville and made their Broadway debut in *Over the Top* in 1917. For the next fifteen years they starred in Broadway and London musicals before Adele married a British aristocrat. Fred appeared on Broadway in *The Gay Divorcee* before going to Hollywood where he was under contract to RKO. He was loaned to MGM and did a musical number with Joan Crawford in *Dancing Lady*. He was teamed with Ginger Rogers and together they appeared in ten successful films. Other films stars who played opposite him were Eleanor Powell, Paulette Goddard, Rita Hayworth, Judy Garland, Leslie Caron, Cyd Charisse, Audrey Hepburn, Ann Miller and Betty Hutton. In 1950 he was awarded a special Oscar for his contribution to films. In 1958, 1959 and 1960 he appeared in television specials in which he danced with Barrie Chase and won many Emmy awards. He put away his dancing shoes in 1959 and continued a successful career as a straight actor. In 1978 he was awarded Kennedy Center Honors for lifetime achievement and in 1981 he received the Life Achievement Award from the American Film Institute. He died at the age of 88 from complications of pneumonia.

Fred Astaire Feature Films (1933–1981)

Dancing Lady (MGM, 1933)
Flying Down to Rio (RKO, 1933)
Roberta (RKO, 1935)
Top Hat (RKO, 1935)
Follow the Fleet (RKO, 1936)

Swing Time (RKO, 1936)
Shall We Dance (RKO, 1937)
A Damsel in Distress (RKO, 1937)
Carefree (RKO, 1938)

Ginger Rogers and Fred Astaire enhanced the hit musical *Follow the Fleet*. It featured Irving Berlin tunes (RKO, 1936).

The Story of Vernon and Irene Castle (RKO, 1939)
Broadway Melody of 1940 (MGM, 1940)
Second Chorus (Par., 1940)
You'll Never Get Rich (Col., 1941)
Holiday Inn (Par., 1942)
You Were Never Lovelier (Col., 1942)

The Sky's the Limit (RKO, 1943)
Yolanda and the Thief (MGM, 1945)
Ziegfeld Follies of 1946 (MGM, 1946)
Blue Skies (Par., 1946)
Easter Parade (MGM, 1948)
The Barkleys of Broadway (MGM, 1949)

Fred Astaire, dressed as the driver of a hansom cab, pursues Ginger Rogers in *Top Hat*. They are caught in the rain, which leads to the song and dance *Isn't It a Lovely Day to Be Caught in the Rain?* (RKO, 1935).

Three Little Words (MGM, 1950)

Let's Dance (Par., 1950)

Royal Wedding (MGM, 1951)

The Belle of New York (MGM, 1952)

The Band Wagon (MGM, 1953)

Deep in My Heart (MGM, 1954)

Daddy Long Legs (20th, 1955)

Funny Face (Par., 1957)

Silk Stockings (MGM, 1957)

On the Beach (UA, 1959)

The Notorious Landlady (Col., 1962)

Finian's Rainbow (WB-7 Arts, 1968)

Midas Run (Cinerama, 1969)

That's Entertainment Part I (MGM, 1974)

The Towering Inferno (20th-WB, 1975)

That's Entertainment Part II (MGM, 1976)

The Amazing Dobermans (Golden Films, 1976)

Un Taxi Mauve (Parafrance, 1977)

Ghost Story (Univ., 1981)

Jackie Cooper, who had outgrown the child roles which made him famous, played the lead in *Dinky*, with Mary Astor cast as his mother (Warner Bros., 1935).

Mary Astor
(1906–1987)

Mary Astor was born in Quincy, Illinois, of a German immigrant father and an American mother who were both teachers. She made her screen debut at the age of fourteen and appeared opposite top stars of the silent era including John Barrymore and Douglas Fairbanks, Sr. With the event of talking pictures she turned to the theatre and won critical success in a play with Edward Everett Horton. She then returned to films. In 1931 her husband, director Kenneth Hawks, died in a plane crash. Her second marriage to Dr. Franklyn Thorpe ended in divorce and a bitter court battle for the custody of their daughter Marylyn. She was one of the organizers of the Screen Actors Guild and served on its board from 1933 to 1936. She married Manuel Martinez

John Huston directed Humphrey Bogart and Mary Astor in *Across the Pacific*, an action-packed adventure about spies in World War II (Warner Bros., 1942).

del Campo and they had a son named Anthony, but that union ended in 1942. In 1945 she married businessman Thomas G. Wheelock and that marriage ended in 1953. She won an Academy Award in 1941 for her performance in *The Great Lie*. She appeared in over one hundred films as well as radio, television and stage productions. She authored five successful novels and two best-selling autobiographies. At eighty-one she died of respiratory failure.

Mary Astor Sound Feature Films (1930–1964)

Ladies Love Brutes (Par., 1930)
The Runaway Bride (RKO, 1930)
Holiday (Pathe, 1930)
The Lash (WB, 1930)
The Sin Ship (RKO, 1930)
The Royal Bed (RKO, 1930)
Other Men's Women (WB, 1931)
Behind Office Doors (RKO, 1931)
White Shoulders (RKO, 1931)
Smart Woman (RKO, 1931)
Men of Chance (RKO, 1931)
The Lost Squadron (RKO, 1932)
A Successful Calamity (WB, 1932)
Those We Love (World Wide, 1932)

Red Dust (MGM, 1932)
The Little Giant (WB, 1933)
Jennie Gerhardt (Par., 1933)
The Kennel Murder Case (WB, 1933)
Convention City (WB, 1933)
The World Changes (WB, 1933)
Easy to Love (WB, 1934)
The Man with Two Faces (WB, 1934)
Return of the Terror (WB, 1934)
Upper World (WB, 1934)
The Case of the Howling Dog (WB, 1934)
I Am a Thief (WB, 1934)
Man of Iron (WB, 1935)
Red Hot Tires (WB, 1935)
Straight from the Heart (Univ., 1935)
Dinky (WB, 1935)
Page Miss Glory (WB, 1935)
The Murder of Dr. Harrigan (WB, 1935)
The Lady from Nowhere (Col., 1936)
And So They Were Married (Col., 1936)
Dodsworth (UA, 1936)
Trapped by Television (Col., 1936)
The Prisoner of Zenda (UA, 1937)
The Hurricane (UA, 1937)
Paradise for Three (MGM, 1938)
No Time to Marry (Col., 1938)
There's Always a Woman (Col., 1938)
Woman Against Woman (MGM, 1938)
Listen, Darling (MGM, 1938)
Midnight (Par., 1939)
Turnabout (UA, 1940)
Brigham Young (20th, 1940)
The Great Lie (WB, 1941)
The Maltese Falcon (WB, 1941)
Across the Pacific (WB, 1942)
In This Our Life (unbilled guest appearance; WB, 1942)
Young Ideas (MGM, 1943)
Meet Me in St. Louis (MGM, 1944)
Blonde Fever (MGM, 1944)
Claudia and David (20th, 1946)
Desert Fury (Par., 1947)
Cynthia (MGM, 1947)
Act of Violence (MGM, 1948)
Cass Timberland (MGM, 1948)
Little Women (MGM, 1949)
Any Number Can Play (MGM, 1949)
A Kiss Before Dying (UA, 1956)
The Power and the Prize (MGM, 1956)
The Devil's Hairpin (Par., 1957)
This Happy Feeling (Univ., 1958)
Stranger in My Arms (Univ., 1959)
Return to Peyton Place (20th, 1961)
Youngblood Hawke (WB, 1964)
Hush ... Hush, Sweet Charlotte (20th, 1964).

Tallulah Bankhead
(1902–1968)

She was the daughter of Congressman William Brockman Bankhead, the Speaker of the House. After winning first prize (a trip to New

Anne Baxter is the lady-in-waiting for Tallulah Bankhead as Catherine the Great in *A Royal Scandal*, directed by Otto Preminger (20th Century–Fox, 1945).

York and a film contract for fifty dollars) in a beauty contest sponsored by *Picture-Play*, she appeared in three films as a bit player. She turned to theatre and made a name for herself in minor roles for four years. The producer, C.B. Cochran, gave her a chance to go to London, and by 1923 her name was up in lights in *The Dancers*. She stayed in London for ten years, lighting up the stage in hit plays. When Paramount signed her she returned to America but her films were disappointing. She returned to Broadway and in 1939 she gave a great performance in Lillian Hellman's *The Little Foxes*. She returned to Hollywood for Alfred Hitchcock's *Lifeboat*, for which she won a New York critics' award. She later extended her appearances to radio, television and summer stock. Her only marriage was to actor John Emery in 1937 and ended in divorce in 1941.

Tallulah Bankhead Sound Film Credits (1931–1966)

Tarnished Lady (Par., 1931)
My Sin (Par., 1931)
The Cheat (Par., 1931)
Thunder Below (Par., 1932)
Make Me a Star (unbilled guest appearance, Par., 1932)
Devil and the Deep (Par., 1932)
Faithless (Par., 1932)
Stage Door Canteen (UA, 1943)

Lifeboat (20th, 1944)
A Royal Scandal (20th, 1945)
Main Street to Broadway (MGM, 1953)
Die! Die! My Darling! (Col., 1965)
The Daydreamer (voice only; Embassy, 1966).

John Barrymore (1882–1942)

He was born in Philadelphia to theatrical parents, Maurice and Georgiana Barrymore. His older brother and sister, Lionel and Ethel Barrymore, also achieved stardom and acclaim. He studied in Paris and planned to be a journalist. He first appeared in the theatre in 1903, then went on to Broadway and then to London. He co-starred with his brother Lionel in the hit *The Jest* in 1919. Then he did Shakespeare's *Richard III* and scored in his greatest triumph as *Hamlet*. He appeared in numerous silent films and made the transition to sound successfully. On screen he appeared with Greta Garbo, Katharine Hepburn, Carole Lombard, Myrna Loy and Claudette Colbert, to name a few. In his last years he returned to the stage in an inferior play which ran 34 weeks in Chicago but failed on Broadway.

John Barrymore Sound Film Credits (1929–1941)

Show of Shows (WB, 1929)
General Crack (WB, 1929)
The Man from Blankley's (WB, 1930)

Moby Dick (WB, 1930)
Svengali (WB, 1931)
Mad Genius (WB, 1931)
Arsene Lupin (MGM, 1932)

Opposite: Alfred Hitchcock's thriller *Lifeboat*, about survivors who climbed aboard a lifeboat after their ship was torpedoed in World War II. *(Listed left to right)* Walter Slezak, John Hodiak, Hume Cronyn, Tallulah Bankhead, Mary Anderson, Heather Angel *(back)*, Henry Hull *(front left)*, and William Bendix *(front right)* (20th Century–Fox, 1944).

Top: John Barrymore plays the part of a royal prince who arrives at court to warn Czar Nicholas II that quick reforms are needed. He is helped by Natasha (Diana Wynyard) in *Rasputin and the Empress* (MGM, 1932). *Bottom:* Reginald Mason *(with handkerchief)* takes John Barrymore and Myrna Loy *(seated)* to lunch where his wife, played by Jobyna Howland, meets them unexpectedly in the comedy *Topaze* (RKO, 1933).

Grand Hotel (MGM, 1932)
State's Attorney (RKO, 1932)
A Bill of Divorcement (RKO, 1932)
Rasputin and the Empress (MGM, 1932)
Topaze (RKO, 1933)
Reunion in Vienna (MGM, 1933)
Dinner at Eight (MGM, 1933)
Night Flight (MGM, 1933)
Counsellor at Law (Univ., 1933)
Long Lost Father (RKO, 1934)
Twentieth Century (Col., 1934)
Romeo and Juliet (MGM, 1936)
Maytime (MGM, 1937)
Bulldog Drummond Comes Back (Par., 1937)
Night Club Scandal (Par., 1937)
True Confession (Par., 1937)
Bulldog Drummond's Revenge (Par., 1937)
Bulldog Drummond's Peril (Par., 1938)
Romance in the Dark (Par., 1938)
Spawn of the North (Par., 1938)
Marie Antoinette (MGM, 1938)
Hold That Co-ed (20th, 1938)
The Great Man Votes (RKO, 1939)
Midnight (Par., 1939)
The Great Profile (20th, 1940)
The Invisible Woman (Univ., 1941)
World Premiere (Par., 1941)
Playmates (RKO, 1941)

Warner Baxter
(1892–1951)

Born in Columbus, Ohio, and raised in San Francisco by his widowed mother, he returned to Columbus after high school to work as a salesman. He worked briefly in vaudeville in Louisville, Kentucky, which led to a job in a touring company and the lead in *Brewster's Millions*. In Los Angeles he joined Morosco's stock company and appeared in silent films with Mae Marsh, Colleen Moore, Florence Vidor, Bebe Daniels, Agnes Ayres and Gilda Grey.

His break came in 1929 when he replaced injured Raoul Walsh in the film *In Old Arizona*. The role won him an Oscar for the year's best male performance.

In the following years he appeared as a star with Joan Bennet, Loretta Young, Janet Gaynor, Myrna Loy, Alice Faye and Ginger Rogers. After an illness which kept him off the screen for two years, he returned with Columbia, where he made grade B films. He lived in Malibu where he was active in civic affairs.

Warner Baxter Sound Film Credits (1929–1950)

In Old Arizona (Fox, 1929)
Through Different Eyes (Fox, 1929)
Behind That Curtain (Fox, 1929)
Romance of the Rio Grande (Fox, 1929)
Happy Days (Fox, 1930)
Such Men Are Dangerous (Fox, 1930)
Arizona Kid (Fox, 1930)
Renegades (Fox, 1930)
Doctor's Wives (Fox, 1931)
Squaw Man (MGM, 1931)
Daddy Long Legs (Fox, 1931)
Their Mad Moment (Fox, 1931)
Cisco Kid (Fox, 1931)
Surrender (Fox, 1931)
Amateur Daddy (Fox, 1932)
Man About Town (Fox, 1932)
Six Hours to Live (Fox, 1932)
Dangerously Yours (Fox, 1933)
42nd Street (WB, 1933)
I Loved You Wednesday (Fox, 1933)
Paddy the Next Best Thing (Fox, 1933)
Penthouse (MGM, 1933)
As Husbands Go (Fox, 1934)
Stand Up and Cheer (Fox, 1934)
Such Women Are Dangerous (Fox, 1934)
Grand Canary (Fox, 1934)
Broadway Bill (Col., 1934)
Hell in the Heavens (Fox, 1934)
One More Spring (Fox, 1935)
Under the Pampas Moon (Fox, 1936)
King of Burlesque (Fox, 1935)
Robin Hood of El Dorado (Fox, 1936)

The Prisoner of Shark Island (20th, 1936)
The Road to Glory (20th, 1936)
To Mary—With Love (20th, 1936)
White Hunter (20th, 1936)
Slave Ship (20th, 1937)
Vogues of 1938 (UA, 1937)
Wife, Doctor and Nurse (20th, 1938)
Kidnapped (20th, 1938)
I'll Give a Million (20th, 1938)
Wife, Husband and Friend (20th, 1939)
Return of the Cisco Kid (20th, 1939)
Barricade (20th, 1939)
Earthbound (20th, 1940)
Adam Had Four Sons (Col., 1941)
Crime Doctor (Col., 1943)
Crime Doctor's Strangest Case (Col., 1943)
Lady in the Dark (Par., 1944)
Shadows in the Night (Col., 1944)
The Crime Doctor's Courage (Col., 1945)
Just Before Dawn (Col., 1946)
The Crime Doctor's Man Hunt (Col., 1946)
The Millerson Case (Col., 1947)
A Gentleman from Nowhere (Col., 1948)
Prison Warden (Col., 1949)
The Devil's Henchman (Col., 1949)
The Crime Doctor's Diary (Col., 1949)
State Penitentiary (Col., 1950)

Top: Dick Powell and Bebe Daniels *(center)* with the chorus line and Warner Baxter *(seated right)* in *42nd Street,* the all-time blockbuster musical with dance numbers staged by Busby Berkeley (Warner Bros., 1933). *Bottom:* Warner Baxter cast as *White Hunter,* an explorer with a troubled past, who is hired by the father of June Lang *(depicted)* to lead an expedition into Africa (20th Century–Fox, 1936).

Wallace Beery
(1885–1949)

Wallace Beery was the younger brother of Noah Beery and uncle of Noah Beery, Jr. He ran away from Kansas City, Missouri, at sixteen and joined Ringling Brothers Circus as an elephant trainer's assistant. Two years later he was in Broadway musicals. He toured in stock before doing comedy shorts in films as Sweedie, a Swedish maid. When he married Gloria Swanson in 1916 he was appearing in featured films as a heavy and in comic roles. He and Swanson divorced two years later. After a time at Paramount he was dropped and MGM signed him. He was cast in a role intended for Lon Chaney, who had died. The picture, *The Big House,* won rave notices. In 1932 he won an Oscar for his performance in *The Champ* and was named one of the year's ten top box office draws.

The studio cast him with Marie Dressler in two hit pictures. After her death he starred in a film with Marjorie Rambeau. Marjorie Main proved herself a worthy co-star in many of his later films. He died of a heart attack in 1949.

Wallace Beery Sound Film Credits (1929–1949)

Chinatown Nights (Par., 1929)
River of Romance (Par., 1929)
Big House (MGM, 1930)
Way for a Sailor (MGM, 1930)
Billy the Kid (MGM, 1930)
A Lady's Morals (MGM, 1930)
Min and Bill (MGM, 1930)
Secret Six (MGM, 1931)
Hell Divers (MGM, 1931)
The Champ (MGM, 1931)
Grand Hotel (MGM, 1932)
Flesh (MGM, 1932)
Dinner at Eight (MGM, 1933)
Tugboat Annie (MGM, 1933)
The Bowery (UA, 1933)
Viva Villa!, (MGM, 1934)

Treasure Island (MGM, 1934)
The Mighty Barnum (UA, 1934)
West Point of the Air (MGM, 1935)
China Seas (MGM, 1935)
O'Shaughnessy's Boy (MGM, 1935)
Ah! Wilderness (MGM, 1936)
A Message to Garcia (20th, 1936)
Old Hutch (MGM, 1936)
Good Old Soak (MGM, 1937)
Slave Ship (20th, 1937)
The Bad Man of Brimstone (MGM, 1938)
Port of Seven Seas (MGM, 1938)

Top: Wallace Beery and Marie Dressler as the lovable couple in *Min and Bill.* They became a favorite screen team. This film was one of 1930's outstanding successes (MGM, 1930). *Bottom:* Wallace Beery in his last film, *Big Jack,* with Marjorie Main as his foil (MGM, 1949).

Stablemates (MGM, 1938)
Stand Up and Fight (MGM, 1939)
Sergeant Madden (MGM, 1939)
Thunder Afloat (MGM, 1939)
The Man from Dakota (MGM, 1940)
20 Mule Team (MGM, 1940)
Wyoming (MGM, 1940)
Barnacle Bill (MGM, 1941)
The Bugle Sounds (MGM, 1941)
Jackass Mail (MGM, 1942)

Salute to the Marines (MGM, 1943)
Rationing (MGM, 1944)
Barbary Coast Gent (MGM, 1944)
This Man's Navy (MGM, 1945)
Bad Bascomb (MGM, 1946)
The Mighty McGurk (MGM, 1946)
Alias a Gentleman (MGM, 1948)
A Date with Judy (MGM, 1948)
Big Jack (MGM, 1949)

Constance Bennett
(1905–1965)

Constance was the oldest of three sisters (Constance, Barbara and Joan) in a famous theatrical family. In 1921 she married Chester Moorehead but the marriage failed. She appeared in silent films and became a star in 1926 under contract with MGM. When she married millionaire Phillip Plant she asked for a release from her contract. After her divorce from Plant she married the Marquis de la Falaise and returned to Hollywood. She made a successful transition from silent films to talkies and retained her status as a star under the guidance of her agent, Myron Selznick. Her third marriage failed and in 1941 she married actor Gilbert Roland. That union ended in 1945.

She appeared on television in the '50s and toured successfully on the stage in Auntie Mame and Toys in the Attic. In 1965 she returned to the screen in a featured role in Ross Hunter's Madame X; within a few months she was dead of a cerebral hemorrhage.

Constance Bennett Sound Film Credits (1929–1966)

This Thing Called Love (Pathé, 1929)
Son of the Gods (WB, 1930)
Rich People (Pathé, 1930)

Common Clay (Fox, 1930)
Three Faces East (WB, 1930)
Sin Takes a Holiday (Pathé, 1930)

Top: Constance Bennett is one of three working girls who pool their savings to rent an expensive apartment in order to impress men they wish to marry. She attracts Paul Lukas in *Ladies in Love* (20th, Century–Fox, 1936). *Bottom: Merrily We Live*, a quick-moving farce from producer Hal Roach. It starred Constance Bennett as an heiress and Brian Ahern as the unexpected suitor (MGM, 1938).

The Easiest Way (MGM, 1931)
The Common Law (RKO, 1931)
Bought (WB, 1931)
Lady with a Past (RKO, 1932)
Two Against the World (WB, 1932)
Rockabye (RKO, 1932)
Our Betters (RKO, 1933)
Bed of Roses (RKO, 1933)
After Tonight (RKO, 1933)
Moulin Rouge (UA, 1934)
Affairs of Cellini (UA, 1934)
Outcast Lady (MGM, 1934)
After Office Hours (MGM, 1935)
Everything Is Thunder (GB, 1936)
Ladies in Love (20th, 1936)
Topper (MGM, 1937)
Merrily We Live (MGM, 1938)
Service De Luxe (Univ., 1938)
Topper Takes a Trip (UA, 1938)

Tail Spin (20th, 1939)
Escape to Glory (Col., 1940)
Law of the Tropics (WB, 1941)
Two-Faced Woman (MGM, 1941)
Wild Bill Hickok Rides (WB, 1941)
Sin Town (Univ., 1942)
Madame Spy (Univ., 1942)
Secret Command (Col., 1944)
Paris Underground (UA, 1945)
Centennial Summer (20th, 1946)
The Unsuspected (WB, 1947)
Smart Woman (AA, 1948)
Angel on the Amazon (Rep., 1949)
As Young as You Feel (20th, 1951)
It Should Happen to You (Col., 1953)
Madame X (Univ., 1966)

Jack Benny
(1894–1974)

After leaving school Benny worked in his father's haberdashery and played the violin in a local band in Waukegan, Illinois. He then went into vaudeville. During World War I he served in the navy and afterward returned to vaudeville and night club work, where he was seen and signed by MGM as a comedian. He made several films for MGM and then asked for a release from his contract. It was granted. His great success came on CBS radio in the '30s with his wife Mary Livingstone and "Rochester" Anderson. Returning to films, he signed with Paramount and great box office hits followed. His greatest success was with Carole Lombard in *To Be or Not to Be,* released by United Artists under the direction of Ernst Lubitsch. His television shows were also successful.

He died in 1974, just before he was to begin one of the leads in the film *The Sunshine Boys,* and George Burns took over the role.

Carole Lombard and Jack Benny play a theatre couple against the backdrop of the Nazis in Poland in *To Be or Not to Be* (United Artists, 1942).

Jack Benny Film Credits (1929–1967)

Hollywood Revue of 1929 (MGM, 1929)

Chasing Rainbows (MGM, 1930)

Medicine Man (Tif., 1930)

Transatlantic Merry-Go-Round (UA, 1934)

Broadway Melody of 1936 (MGM, 1935)

It's in the Air (MGM, 1935)

The Big Broadcast of 1937 (Par., 1936)

College Holiday (Par., 1936)

Artists and Models (Par., 1937)

Gracie Allen tells Jack Benny *(center)* and George Burns that her uncle has invented a television device in *The Big Broadcast of 1937* (Paramount, 1936).

Artists and Models Abroad (Par., 1938)
Man About Town (Par., 1939)
Buck Benny Rides Again (Par., 1940)
Love Thy Neighbor (Par., 1940)
Charley's Aunt (20th, 1941)
To Be or Not to Be (UA, 1942)
George Washington Slept Here (WB, 1942)
The Meanest Man in the World (20th, 1943)
Hollywood Canteen (WB, 1944)
It's in the Bag (UA, 1945)
The Horn Blows at Midnight (WB, 1945)
Without Reservations (unbilled guest appearance; RKO, 1946)
The Great Lover (unbilled guest appearance; Par., 1949)
Somebody Loves Me (unbilled guest appearance; Par., 1952)
Susan Slept Here (unbilled guest appearance; RKO, 1954)
Beau James (unbilled guest appearance; Par., 1957)
Gypsy (unbilled guest appearance; WB, 1962)
It's a Mad, Mad, Mad, Mad World (unbilled guest appearance; UA, 1963), *A Guide for the Married Man"* (20th, 1967).

Ingrid Bergman
(1915–1982)

Born in Stockholm, Sweden, and orphaned at an early age, she was raised by relatives on an inheritance from her father. After graduating from high school, she enrolled at Stockholm's Royal Dramatic Theatre. She married Dr. Peter Lindstrom who encouraged her to enter films. After one year of playing small roles, she was elevated to leading roles and gained an international reputation.

David O. Selznick signed her to a seven-year contract. Her first Selznick film was *Intermezzo*, which she had made in Sweden several years before. She made her Broadway debut in a revival of *Liliom*. Several films followed on loan-out. *Casablanca* at Warner Brothers with Humphrey Bogart was memorable and a box office smash. Other outstanding vehicles followed and she became a box office champion.

Ingrid Bergman

She left Selznick and was less successful as a free-lancer. After her divorce from Linstrom in 1950 she married Roberto Rosselini and went to Europe to live and work. Their marriage ended in 1958.

She returned to the stage, appearing in Paris, London and New York, and toured the United States with occasional films. Her last marriage was to Lars Schmidt, a Swedish stage producer.

Miss Bergman won two Academy Awards for best leading actress in *Gaslight* and *Anastasia* and was chosen best supporting actress in *Murder on the Orient Express*. She also won an Emmy for her television performance in *A Woman Called Golda*.

Top: Ingrid Bergman made her debut with Leslie Howard in *Intermezzo*, produced by David O. Selznick under the expert direction of Gregory Ratoff (United Artists, 1939). *Bottom:* Humphrey Bogart saying goodbye to Ingrid Bergman with the famous line "Here's looking at you, kid" in *Casablanca* (Warner Bros., 1942).

Ingrid Bergman Film Credits (1939–1979)

Intermezzo (UA, 1939)

Adam Had Four Sons (Col., 1941)

Rage in Heaven (MGM, 1941)

Dr. Jeckyll and Mr. Hyde (MGM, 1941)

Casablanca (WB, 1942)

For Whom the Bell Tolls (Par., 1943)

Gaslight (MGM, 1944)

Spellbound (UA, 1945)

Saratoga Trunk (WB, 1945)

The Bells of St. Mary's (RKO, 1946)

Notorious (RKO, 1946)

Arch of Triumph (UA, 1948)

Joan of Arc (RKO, 1948)

Under Capricorn (WB, 1949)

Strangers (Fine Arts, 1955)

Anastasia (20th, 1956)

Indiscreet (WB, 1958)

The Inn of the Sixth Happiness (20th, 1958)

Goodbye Again (UA, 1961)

The Visit (20th, 1964)

The Yellow Rolls-Royce (MGM, 1965)

Stimulantia (Swedish, 1967)

Fugitive in Vienna (WB, 1968)

Cactus Flower (Col., 1969)

A Walk in the Spring Rain (Col., 1970)

From the Mixed-Up Files of Mrs. Basil E. Frankweiler (Cinema 5, 1974)

Murder on the Orient Express (Par., 1974)

A Matter of Time (AIP, 1976)

Autumn Sonata (Sweden, 1979)

Humphrey Bogart
(1899–1957)

Bogart, whose father was a physician, was born in New York City. During World War I he enlisted in the navy and was wounded in battle. After his discharge he became interested in the theatre. He began his career with William A. Brady as an office boy and worked up to stage manager. During the '20s he switched to acting. He made a ten-minute short which led to a contract with Fox. He appeared in films with Spencer Tracy, Bette Davis and Victor McLaglen but his Fox option was dropped and he returned to Broadway. In 1935 he was cast in Robert E. Sherwood's play *The Petrified Forest* starring Leslie Howard. When the film version was made Bogart repeated the role of Duke Mantee. Under contract to Warner Brothers from 1936 to 1940, he appeared in numerous films. After several other actors had turned down the lead in *High Sierra,* he played it under the direction of Raoul Walsh and became a star in his own right.

Humphrey Bogart as "Mad Dog Ray Earle" and Ida Lupino as the gangster's moll gave one of their finest performances in *High Sierra* (Warner, 1941).

In 1945 he married Lauren Bacall and they had two children. He formed his own company, Santana Pictures, with himself as producer.

In 1951 he won an Academy Award for the lead in *African Queen* with Katharine Hepburn as co-star and John Huston as director.

Humphrey Bogart Film Credits (1930–1956)

Broadways Like That (WB, 1930)

A Devil with Women (Fox, 1930)

Up the River (Fox, 1930)

Body and Soul (Fox, 1931)

Bad Sister Univ., 1931)

Women of All Nations (Fox, 1931)

A Holy Terror (Fox, 1931)

Love Affair (Col., 1932)

Three on a Match (WB, 1932)

Midnight (Univ., 1934)

Top: Battle Circus tells the story of a nurse, June Allyson, who comes to Korea to serve at Humphrey Bogart's Mobile Army Surgical Corps, and Robert Keith *(center)*, who appears as Lt. Col. Hillary Whalters (MGM, 1953). *Bottom:* Humphrey Bogart *(left)* as private detective Sam Spade examines *The Maltese Falcon* as Peter Lorre, Mary Astor and Sydney Greenstreet look on greedily (Warner Bros., 1941).

The Petrified Forest (WB, 1936)
Two Against the World (WB, 1936)
Bullets or Ballots (WB, 1936)
China Clipper (WB, 1936)
Isle of Fury (WB, 1936)
The Great O'Malley (WB, 1937)
Black Legion (WB, 1937)
San Quentin (WB, 1937)
Marked Woman (WB, 1937)
Kid Galahad (WB, 1937)
Dead End (UA, 1937)
Stand-In (UA, 1937)
Swing Your Lady (WB, 1938)
Men Are Such Fools (WB, 1938)
The Amazing Dr. Clitterhouse (WB, 1938)
Racket Busters (WB, 1938)
Angels with Dirty Faces (WB, 1938)
King of the Underworld (WB, 1939)
The Oklahoma Kid (WB, 1939)
Dark Victory (WB, 1939)
You Can't Get Away with Murder (WB, 1939)
The Roaring Twenties (WB, 1939)
The Return of Dr. X (WB, 1939)
Invisible Stripes (WB, 1939)
Virginia City (WB, 1940)
It All Came True (WB, 1940)
Brother Orchid (WD, 1940)
They Drive By Night (WB, 1940)
High Sierra (WB, 1941)
The Wagons Roll at Night (WB, 1941)
The Maltese Falcon (WB, 1941)
All Through the Night (WB, 1942)
The Big Shot (WB, 1942)
In This Our Life (unbilled guest appearance; WB, 1942)
Across the Pacific (WB, 1942)
Casablanca (WB, 1942)

Action in the North Atlantic (WB, 1943)
Thank Your Lucky Stars (WB, 1943)
Sahara (Col., 1943)
To Have and Have Not (WB, 1944)
Passage to Marseille (WB, 1944)
Conflict (WB, 1945)
The Big Sleep (WB, 1946)
Two Guys from Milwaukee (unbilled guest appearance; WB, 1946)
The Two Mrs. Carrolls (WB, 1947)
Dead Reckoning (Col., 1947)
Dark Passage (WB, 1947)
Treasure of the Sierra Madre (WB, 1948)
Key Largo (WB, 1948)
It's a Great Feeling (WB, 1949)
Knock on Any Door (Col., 1949)
Tokyo Joe (Col., 1949)
Chain Lightning (WB, 1950)
In a Lonely Place (Col., 1950)
The Enforcer (WB, 1951)
Sirocco (Col., 1951)
The African Queen (UA, 1952)
Deadline—USA (20th, 1952)
Battle Circus (MGM, 1953)
Beat the Devil (UA, 1954)
The Caine Mutiny (Col., 1954)
Sabrina (Par., 1954)
The Barefoot Contessa (UA, 1954)
Love Lottery (unbilled guest appearance; Rank, 1954)
We're No Angels (Par., 1955)
The Left Hand of God (20th, 1955)
The Desperate Hours (Par., 1955)
The Harder They Fall (Col., 1956)

Charles Boyer is a Czech author who flees from the Nazis to England and meets Jennifer Jones, a maid who is also a plumber, in *Cluny Brown* (20th Century–Fox, 1946).

Charles Boyer
(1899–1978)

Charles Boyer was born in Figeac, France, attended the Sorbonne and studied drama at the Paris Conservatoire. After only a few years on the Paris stage he became a star. He came to the U.S. under contract to MGM and made two French editions of Hollywood hits. On loan to Paramount he did one film with Ruth Chatterton and another with Claudette Colbert. Dissatisfied with Hollywood, he returned to France and made films there. Several years later he returned to Hollywood and pursued a successful careeer opposite such stars as Loretta Young, Claudette Colbert, Marlene Dietrich, Jean Arthur, Greta Garbo, and Ingrid Bergman from 1934 to 1948. He then alternated between the U.S. and Europe, where he appeared in films with Michele Morgan, Lilian

Charles Boyer and Marsha Hunt are the parents of a twelve-year-old boy who develops an attraction to the opposite sex in *The Happy Time* (Columbia, 1952).

Harvey, Danielle Darrieux and Sophia Loren. His marriage in 1934 to English actress Pat Patterson lasted until her death in 1978.

On Broadway he did *Red Gloves* in 1948, *King Sir* with Mary Martin in 1953 and *The Marriage Go-Round* with Claudette Colbert in 1958. On U.S. television he starred in *There Shall Be No Night* with Katharine Cornell and appeared on *Four Star Playhouse* and the series *The Rogues*.

He continued making films in Hollywood and Europe until his death in 1978.

Charles Boyer English-Speaking Feature Films (1932–1976)

Red-Headed Woman (MGM, 1932)
The Man from Yesterday (Par., 1932)
The Only Girl (GB, 1933)
Caravan (Fox, 1934)
Thunder in the East (UA, 1934)
Private Worlds Par., 1935)

Shanghai (Par., 1935)
Break of Hearts (RKO, 1935)
The Garden of Allah (UA, 1936)
Tavarich (WB, 1937)
Conquest (MGM, 1937)
History Is Made at Night (UA, 1937)
Algiers (UA, 1938)

Love Affair (RKO, 1939)
When Tomorrow Comes (Univ., 1939)
All This, and Heaven, Too (WB, 1940)
Hold Back the Dawn (Par., 1941)
Back Street (Univ., 1941)
Appointment for Love (Univ., 1941)
Tales of Manhattan (20th, 1942)
The Heart of a Nation (narrator; AFE, 1943)
The Constant Nymph (WB, 1943)
Flesh and Fantasy (Univ., 1943)
Gaslight (MGM, 1944)
Together Again (Col., 1944)
Confidential Agent (WB, 1945)
Cluny Brown (20th, 1946)
A Woman's Vengeance (Univ., 1947)
Arch of Triumph (UA, 1948)
The First Legion (UA, 1951)
The Thirteenth Letter (20th, 1951)

The Happy Time (Col., 1952)
Thunder in the East (Par., 1953)
The Cobweb (MGM, 1955)
Around the World in 80 Days (UA, 1956)
The Buccaneer (Par., 1958)
Fanny (WB, 1961)
The Four Horsemen of the Apocalypse (MGM, 1962)
Love Is a Ball (UA, 1963)
A Very Special Favor (Univ., 1965)
How to Steal a Million (20th, 1966)
Is Paris Burning? (Par., 1966)
Casino Royale (Col., 1967)
Barefoot in the Park (Par., 1967)
The Day the Hot Line Got Hot (AIP, 1968)
April Fools (NGP, 1969)
Madwoman of Chaillot (WB, 1969)
Lost Horizon (Col., 1973)
Matter of Time (AIP, 1976)

George Brent
(1904–1979)

George Brent was born in Shennonsbridge, Ireland. He was orphaned at the age of eleven and was sent to the U.S. to live with relatives. When he reached college age he returned to Ireland to attend Dublin University and acted at the Abbey Theatre. Due to his subversive activities during the Irish Rebellion he was forced to flee to Canada. He joined a stock company there and toured for two years. He then went to New York and worked in several stock companies before making his Broadway debut in the late '20s. He went to Hollywood as a contract player and became a U.S. citizen in 1934. Under contract to Warner Brothers and on loan to other studios he appeared opposite Greta Garbo, Hedy Lamarr, Ginger Rogers, Barbara Stanwyck, Myrna

George Brent

Loy, Kay Francis and Olivia de Havilland. He appeared in eleven films with Bette Davis. As a licensed pilot he tried to join the armed forces during World War II but was rejected because of his age. When he retired from films he ran a horse breeding ranch but returned occasionally to films. He died in 1979 of emphysema.

George Brent Sound Films (1930–1956)

Under Suspicion (Fox, 1930)
Lightning Warrior (Mascot serial, 1931)
Once a Sinner (Fox, 1931)
Fair Warning (Fox, 1931)
Charlie Chan Carries On (Fox, 1931)
Ex-Bad Boy (Univ., 1931)
So Big (WB, 1932)
The Rich Are Always with Us (WB, 1932)
Week-End Marriage (WB, 1932)
Miss Pinkerton (WB, 1932)
Purchase Price (WB, 1932)
The Crash (WB, 1932)
They Call It Sin (WB, 1932)
Luxury Liner (Par., 1933)
42nd Street (WB, 1933)
The Keyhole (WB, 1933)
Female (WB, 1933)
Lilly Turner (WB, 1933)
Baby Face (WB, 1933)

In This Our Life was adapted from Ellen Glasgow's Pulitzer Prize–winning novel, with Bette Davis *(left)* as the spoiled and selfish sister and Olivia de Havilland as the good sister in love with George Brent (Warner Bros., 1942).

Stamboul Quest (MGM, 1934)
Housewife (WB, 1934)
Desirable (WB, 1934)
The Painted Veil (MGM, 1934)
Living on Velvet (WB, 1935)
Stranded (WB, 1935)
Front Page Woman (WB, 1935)
The Goose and the Gander (WB, 1935)
Special Agent (WB, 1935)
In Person (RKO, 1935)
The Right to Live (WB, 1936)
Snowed Under (WB, 1936)
The Golden Arrow (WB, 1936)
The Case Against Mrs. Ames (Par., 1936)
Give Me Your Heart (WB, 1936)
More Than a Secretary (Col., 1936)
God's Country and the Woman (WB, 1936)
The Go-Getter (WB, 1937)
Mountain Justice (WB, 1937)
Submarine D-1 (WB, 1937)
Gold Is Where You Find It (WB, 1938)
Jezebel (WB, 1938)
Racket Busters (WB, 1938)
Secrets of an Actress (WB, 1938)
Wings of the Navy (WB, 1939)
Dark Victory (WB, 1939)
Old Maid (WB, 1939)
The Rains Came (20th, 1939)
The Man Who Talked Too Much (WB, 1940)
South of Suez (WB, 1940)
Honeymoon for Three (WB, 1941)
The Great Lie (WB, 1941)
They Dare Not Love (Col., 1941)
International Lady (UA, 1941)

In This Our Life (WB, 1942)
Twin Beds (UA, 1942)
The Gay Sisters (WB, 1942)
You Can't Escape Forever (WB, 1942)
Silver Queen (UA, 1942)
The Affairs of Susan (Par., 1945)
Experiment Perilous (RKO, 1945)
My Reputation (WB, 1946)
The Spiral Staircase (RKO, 1946)
Tomorrow Is Forever (RKO, 1946)
Lover Come Back (Univ., 1946)
Temptation (Univ., 1946)
Slave Girl (Univ., 1947)
Out of the Blue (EL, 1947)

The Corpse Came C.O.D. (Col., 1947)
Christmas Eve (UA, 1947)
Luxury Liner (MGM, 1948)
Angel on the Amazon (Rep., 1948)
Red Canyon (Univ., 1949)
Illegal Entry (Univ., 1949)
Kid from Cleveland (Rep., 1949)
Bride for Sale (RKO, 1949)
FBI Girl (Lip., 1951)
Main Bait (Lip., 1952)
Montana Belle (RKO, 1952)
Tangier Incident (AA, 1953)
Death of a Scoundrel (RKO, 1956)

Joe E. Brown
(1892–1973)

At an age of nine Brown ran away from his home in Holgate, Ohio, to join a circus as an acrobat in an aerial act. Years later he broke his leg during a performance and turned to stage and vaudeville acting. In 1920 he made his Broadway debut in *Jim Jam Jems.* This and other successes were followed by tours in *Elmer the Great* and *Square Crooks.* He first appeared in movies in the silent film *Crooks Can't Wait* in 1927. In 1929 he signed a contract with Warner Brothers which lasted until 1944.

During World War II he did 742 overseas shows and won the Bronze Star for his outstanding efforts. He played the lead in *Harvey* in more than 2,000 performances over a five-year period in the U.S., London and Australia.

He wrote two books, *Your Kids and Mine* and *Laughter Is a Wonderful Thing.* He then returned to the screen in a cameo role for Mike Todd in *Around the World in 80 Days* and a guest role in *Some Like It Hot* for Billy Wilder.

He passed away after a long illness at the age of 82 with his family at his bedside.

Top: Joe E. Brown stars as a tractor salesman who can sell *Earthworm Tractors* to anybody including Carol Hughes (First National, 1936). *Bottom:* Joe E. Brown, a cub reporter on his uncle's newspaper, uncovers a plot to kill an aged archduke played by Harry Davenport *(far right).* He saves both the archduke and the princess, Helen Mack, with thanks given to Robert Warwick in *Fit for a King* (RKO, 1937).

Joe E. Brown Sound Film Credits (1929–1963)

On With the Show (WB, 1929)
Painted Faces (Tif., 1930)
Song of the West (WB, 1930)
Hold Everything (WB, 1930)
Top Speed (WB, 1930)
Lottery Bride (UA, 1930)
Maybe It's Love (WB, 1930)
Going Wild (WB, 1931)
Sit Tight (WB, 1931)
Broad Minded (WB, 1931)
Local Boy Makes Good (WB, 1931)
Fireman Save My Child (WB, 1932)
The Tenderfoot (WB, 1932)
You Said a Mouthful (WB, 1932)
Elmer the Great (WB, 1933)
Son of a Sailor (WB, 1933)
A Very Honorable Guy (WB, 1934)
Circus Clown (WB, 1934)
Alibi Ike (WB, 1935)
Bright Lights (WB, 1935)
A Midsummer Night's Dream (WB, 1935)
Sons o' Guns (WB, 1936)

Earthworm Tractors (WB, 1936)
Polo Joe (WB, 1936)
When's Your Birthday? (RKO, 1937)
Riding on Air (RKO, 1937)
Fit for a King (RKO, 1937)
Wide Open Faces (Col., 1938)
Flirting with Fate (MGM, 1938)
The Gladiator (Col., 1938)
$1000 a Touchdown (Par., 1939)
Beware Spooks! (Col., 1939)
So You Won't Talk (Col., 1940)
Shut My Big Mouth (Col., 1942)
Joan of the Ozarks (Rep., 1942)
Chatterbox (Rep., 1943)
Casanova in Burlesque (Rep., 1944)
Pin-Up Girl (20th, 1944)
Hollywood Canteen (WB, 1944)
The Tender Years (20th, 1947)
Show Boat (MGM, 1951)
Around the World in 80 Days (UA, 1956)
Some Like It Hot (UA, 1959)
The Comedy of Terrors (AIP, 1963)

James Cagney
(1899–1986)

James Cagney was born July 17, 1899, in New York City. He worked his way through high school and one semester at Columbia University doing various jobs from wrapping packages in a department store to taking tickets on a tour boat. In his teens he was a runner-up for the New York State lightweight amateur boxing title and took part in amateur theatricals at Lenox Hill Settlement House. Without any dancing training he auditioned for a chorus job and was hired only because he picked up steps easily. While appearing in *Pitter Patter* in 1922 he married

James Cagney

Frances Willard Vernon, also a member of the chorus. Together they toured the vaudeville circuit. Then Cagney began his acting career in various plays on Broadway. In two of these he co-starred with Joan Blondell. The second one, *Penny Arcade*, directed by William Keighley, was sold to Warner Brothers. The title was changed to *Sinner's Holiday* in which both Cagney and Blondell repeated their *Penny Arcade* roles on film. Under contract to Warner he played various roles before he

James Cagney plays Chicago gangster Tom Powers, who smashes a grapefruit into Mae Clarke's face because of her endless chatter in *Public Enemy* (Warner Bros., 1931).

became a star playing a hoodlum in *Public Enemy* (1931). From that time until his retirement in 1961 Cagney was a top star. He made a total of 64 films and won an Oscar for his portrayal of George M. Cohan in *Yankee Doodle Dandy*. In 1980 he came out of retirement to appear in the film *Ragtime* and in 1983 he did the television film *The Terrible Joe Moran*.

Among his many honors were the Life Achievement Award of the American Film Institute (1974), the Citation for Career Achievement by the John F. Kennedy Center for Performing Arts (1980) and the U.S. Medal of Freedom (1980).

James Cagney Film Credits (1930–1981)

Sinner's Holiday (WB, 1930)
Doorway to Hell (WB, 1930)
Other Men's Women (WB, 1931)
The Millionaire (WB, 1931)
Public Enemy (WB, 1931)

Smart Money (WB, 1931)
Blonde Crazy (WB, 1931)
Taxi (WB, 1932)
The Crowd Roars (WB, 1932)
Winner Take All (WB, 1932)

James Cagney is a struggling dentist trying to made ends meet at the turn of the century. Alan Hale plays his unemployed father in *The Strawberry Blonde* (Warner Bros., 1941).

Hard to Handle (WB, 1933)
Picture Snatcher (WB, 1933)
Footlight Parade (WB, 1933)
Lady Killer (WB, 1933)
Jimmy the Gent (WB, 1934)
He Was Her Man (WB, 1934)
Here Comes the Navy (WB, 1934)
St. Louis Kid (WB, 1934)
Devil Dogs of the Air (WB, 1935)
G-Men (WB, 1935)
The Irish in Us (WB, 1935)
A Midsummer Night's Dream (WB, 1935)
Frisco Kid (WB, 1935)
Ceiling Zero (WB, 1935)
Great Guy (GN, 1936)
Something to Sing About (GN, 1937)

Boy Meets Girl (WB, 1938)
Each Dawn I Die (WB, 1939)
The Roaring Twenties (WB, 1939)
The Fighting 69th (WB, 1940)
Torrid Zone (WB, 1940)
City for Conquest (WB, 1940)
Strawberry Blonde (WB, 1941)
The Bride Came C.O.D. (WB, 1941)
Captain of the Clouds (WB, 1942)
Yankee Doodle Dandy (WB, 1942)
Johnny Come Lately (UA, 1943)
Blood on the Sun (UA, 1945)
13 Rue Madeleine (20th, 1946)
The Time of Your Life (UA, 1948)
White Heat (WB, 1949)

West Point Story (WB, 1950)
Kiss Tomorrow Goodbye (WB, 1950)
Come Fill the Cup (WB, 1951)
Starlift (WB, 1951)
What Price Glory (20th, 1952)
A Lion Is in the Streets (WB, 1953)
Run for Cover (Par., 1955)
Leave Me or Leave Me (MGM, 1955)
Seven Little Boys (Par., 1955)
Mister Roberts (WB, 1955)
Tribute to a Bad Man (MGM, 1956)
These Wilder Years (MGM, 1956)
Man of a Thousand Faces (Univ., 1957)
Never Steal Anything Small (Univ., 1959)
Shake Hands with the Devil (UA, 1959)
The Gallant Hours (UA, 1960)
One, Two, Three! (UA, 1961)
Arizona Buckwhackers (narrator; Par., 1968)
Ragtime (Par., 1981)

Eddie Cantor
(1892–1964)

Cantor was born in New York City to Lower East Side immigrants and was orphaned at an early age. Working days as an office boy, he gained stage experience by night in amateur shows. He appeared for a while in burlesque, then in Gus Edwards' *Kid Kabaret*, followed by a musical revue, *Not Likely*, in London. After returning to the States, his first Broadway appearance was a success and Ziegfeld hired him for the *Follies* of 1917, 1918 and 1919. He left Ziegfeld, worked successfully for producers, and returned to do Ziegfeld's *Kid Boots*. It had a lengthy run and was made into a silent film with Clara Bow. He came back to Broadway under Ziegfeld.

His last vehicle, *Whoopee*, was sold to Samuel Goldwyn and a successful movie was made from it. After many popular films under Goldwyn, he worked for other studios as well. He had also become a radio star.

In 1956 he was given a special award by The Academy of Motion Picture Arts and Sciences for distinguished service to the film industry. He authored four autobiographies and appeared successfully in television.

Top: Eddie Cantor *(right)* inherits seventy-seven million dollars from his archaeologist father. Ethel Merman and Warren Hymer are his friends in *Kid Millions* (United Artists, 1934). *Bottom:* Eddie Cantor *(center)* is mistaken for a bank robber and jailed in Mexico. Leo Willis talks to the jailor (Julian Rivero) as J. Carroll Naish stands in his cell in *The Kid from Spain* (United Artists, 1932).

Eddie Cantor Film Credits (1929–1953)

Glorifying the American Girl (Par., 1929)
Whoopee (UA, 1930)
Palmy Days (UA, 1931)
The Kid from Spain (UA, 1932)
Roman Scandals (UA, 1933)
Kid Millions (UA, 1934)
Strike Me Pink (UA, 1936)
Ali Baba Goes to Town (20th, 1937)
Forty Little Mothers (MGM, 1940)
Thank Your Lucky Stars (WB, 1943),
Hollywood Canteen (WB, 1944)
Show Business (RKO, 1944)
If You Knew Susie (RKO 1948)
The Story of Will Rogers (WB, 1952)
The Eddie Cantor Story (WB, 1953)

Madeleine Carroll
(1906–1987)

Madeleine Carroll was born in West Bromwich, England. She graduated from Birmingham University and became a French teacher. She then did fashion modeling briefly before making her London stage debut in 1927. She appeared in several silent films, made a successful transition to the talkies and became the most popular actress in British films. Under the direction of Alfred Hitchcock she became an international star in two films and then went to Hollywood under contract to Walter Wanger and 20th Century–Fox. After that successful contract ended she signed one with Paramount in 1939 and made more big box office pictures. In 1942 she gave up her screen career and served as a nurse for the U.S. Red Cross in Europe during World War II. She earned the rank of captain and received the Medal of Freedom. In 1946 France awarded her the Legion of Honor. After the war she made her Broadway debut in *Goodbye, My Fancy* which won rave reviews from critics. After the play closed she returned to Hollywood and made only two films before retiring. She had four unsuccessful marriages to Philip Ashley, Sterling Hayden, Henry Lavorel and Andrew Heiskell. The last twenty years of her life were spent in Marbella, Spain, working for charities such as the Red Cross.

Francis Lederer, a rich playboy, disguises himself as a male secretary to protect heiress Madeleine Carroll from a fortune hunter in the comedy *It's All Yours* (Columbia, 1938).

Madeleine Carroll Feature Films (1928–1949)

Guns at Loos (New Era, 1928)

What Money Can't Buy (Par., 1929)

The American Prisoner (BIP, 1929)

Atlantic (BIP, 1930)

Young Woodley (BIP, 1930)

Escape (ETP, 1930)

The "W" Plan (Burlington, 1931)

Mme. Guillotine (Fogwell, 1931)

Kissing Cup's Race (Butchers, 1931)

French Leave (Talking Picture Epics, 1931)

Fascination (BP, 1932)

First Born (Gainsborough, 1932)

School for Scandal (Par., 1933)

Madeleine Carroll is cast as a Belgian nurse who becomes a spy in World War I. Her co-star is Herbert Marshall in *I Was a Spy* (Fox, 1934).

I Was a Spy (Fox, 1934)	*Honeymoon in Bali* (Par., 1939)
The World Moves On (Fox, 1934)	*Cafe Society* (Par., 1939)
Loves of a Dictator (GB, 1935)	*My Son, My Son* (UA, 1940)
The 39 Steps (GB, 1935)	*Safari* (Par., 1940)
The Case Against Mrs. Ames (Par., 1936)	*North West Mounted Police* (Par., 1940)
Secret Agent (GB, 1936)	*Virginia* (Par., 1941)
The General Died at Dawn (Par., 1936)	*One Night in Lisbon* (Par., 1941)
Lloyds of London (20th, 1936)	*Bahama Passage* (Par., 1941)
On the Avenue (20th, 1937)	*My Favorite Blonde* (Par., 1942)
The Prisoner of Zenda (UA, 1937)	*White Cradle Inn* ("High Fury," UA, 1947)
It's All Yours (Col., 1938)	*An Innocent Affair* ("Don't Trust Your Husband," UA, 1948)
Blockade (UA, 1938)	*The Fan* (Fox, 1949)

Charlie Chaplin
(1889–1977)

Charlie Chaplin

Charlie Chaplin was born to English music-hall entertainers. His father died when he was a young child and his mother suffered a breakdown. As a child he danced in the streets for money until he was placed in an orphanage. After a time he joined a troupe of child dancers. He appeared on the London stage in children's parts. Working with the troupe of Fred Karno, a popular comic, gave him the opportunity to acquire comic skills. While touring the U.S. with this troupe, he was seen and hired by Mack Sennett, producer of Keystone movie comedies. Under Keystone's banner he made 35 films. He worked successfully for other studios and in 1919 founded United Artists Corporation with Mary Pickford, Douglas Fairbanks, Sr., and D.W. Griffith.

In its first year of existence (1927–28) the Motion Picture Academy gave him a special award for versatility and genius in writing, acting, directing and producing *The Circus*. In 1935 during the early talkies he

Top: Paulette Goddard is a Jewish laundress in love with Charlie Chaplin, a barber. They escape to Austria in *The Great Dictator.* Charlie also plays the role of Hynkel, a dictator (United Artists, 1940). *Bottom:* Buster Keaton *(left)* watches Charlie Chaplin, a one-time great of British music halls at the turn of the century, as he applies makeup before his final appearance in *Limelight* (United Artists, 1952).

made two successful silent films, *City Lights* and *Modern Times* which introduced Paulette Goddard. His last success in this era was *The Great Dictator* in 1940.

Because of political forces he moved to Europe in 1952 with his fourth wife, Oona O'Neill, and settled in Switzerland. A special Oscar was presented to him in 1975 and he was knighted by the Queen.

Charlie Chaplin Sound Films (1940–1967)

The Great Dictator (UA, 1940)
Monsieur Verdoux (UA, 1947)
Limelight (UA, 1952)

A King in New York (UA, 1957)
A Countess from Hong Kong
(Univ., 1967).

Montgomery Clift (1920–1966)

Montgomery Clift was born in Omaha, Nebraska. He had a twin sister, Ethel, and an older brother, William Brooks, Jr. The family moved first to Chicago and then to New York where his father was a stockbroker. As a teenager he gained stage experience in stock companies in Sarasota, Florida, and Stockbridge, Massachusetts. He made his Broadway debut in 1935 with Thomas Mitchell in *Fly Away Home.* Other Broadway appearances led to a role in Robert Sherwood's Pulitzer-Prize play *There Shall Be No Night* which ran for two seasons, 1940–41, starring the Lunts. He turned down Hollywood offers of seven-year contracts while appearing on stage in *The Skin of Our Teeth*, a revival of *Our Town*, Lillian Hellman's *The Searching Wind, Foxhole in the Parlor* and Tennessee Williams' and Donald Windham's *You Touched Me.* Howard Hawks saw him on stage and hired him to play one of the leads in *Red River*. Clift never signed with any studio, selecting instead his own roles at various studios. He was nominated for best actor by the Academy of Motion Picture Arts and Sciences in 1948 (*The Search*), 1951 (*A Place in the Sun*), and 1953 (*From Here to Eternity*) but he never won. His last movie, *The Defector*, was filmed in Germany. Before its release he died at age 46 in New York.

Top: The James Jones novel *From Here to Eternity* told of pre–World War II enlisted men, their women, and their grim destiny. Donna Reed plays a hostess at the New Congress Club and Montgomery Clift is the rebellious enlisted man (Columbia, 1953). *Bottom:* Montgomery Clift is a reporter who is appointed letters-to-the-lovelorn columnist by publisher Robert Ryan *(right)*. Myrna Loy plays Clift's wife in *Lonelyhearts* (United Artists, 1959).

Montgomery Clift Feature Films (1948–1966)

The Search (MGM, 1948)
Red River (UA, 1948)
The Heiress (Par., 1949)
The Big Lift (20th, 1950)
A Place in the Sun (Par., 1951)
I Confess (WB, 1953)
From Here to Eternity (Col., 1953)
Indiscretion of an American Wife (Col., 1954)
Raintree County (MGM, 1957)

The Young Lions (20th, 1958)
Lonelyhearts (UA, 1959)
Suddenly, Last Summer (Col., 1959)
Wild River (20th, 1960)
The Misfits (UA, 1961)
Judgment at Nuremberg (UA, 1961)
Freud (Univ., 1962)
The Defector (7 Arts, 1966)

Ronald Colman
(1891–1958)

Orphaned at sixteen, he worked in the office of a steamship company for five years. During that time he acted in community theatre. He served in World War I and after the war he gained experience as an actor on the stage and in films. In 1920 he came to the U.S. Lillian Gish saw him in a play starring Ruth Chatterton and selected him to appear opposite her in *The White Sister*. He signed a contract with Samuel Goldwyn and began a successful career in the silent movies. He appeared with Barbara LaMarr, Doris Kenyon, Constance Talmadge, Irene Rich and Velma Banky, all popular actresses of the silent era. With the advent of sound films in 1929, his first film, *Bulldog Drummond,* was a great success. So were many other films which followed under the Goldwyn banner.

After leaving Goldwyn, he signed with 20th Century–Fox and made several successful films. Then he became a free-lance actor and worked for Columbia, Metro-Goldwyn-Mayer, Paramount, RKO Radio and Universal. He won an Oscar for his role in *A Double Life* after being nominated three times previously. He married actress Benita Hume. They did guest appearances on the Jack Benny Show and later had a successful television series, *The Halls of Ivy.*

Under Frank Capra's direction Ronald Colman is the gallant British diplomat who is kidnapped and taken to Shangri-La in *Lost Horizon*. There he meets Jane Wyatt, a resident of that unknown land hidden in the Himalayas (Columbia, 1937).

Ronald Colman Sound Films (1929–1957)

Bulldog Drummond (UA, 1929)
Condemned (UA, 1929)
Raffles (UA, 1930)
The Devil to Pay (UA, 1930)
The Unholy Garden (UA, 1931)
Arrowsmith (UA, 1931)
Cynara (UA, 1932)
The Masquerader (UA, 1933)
Bulldog Drummond Strikes Back (UA, 1934)
Clive of India (UA, 1935)
The Man Who Broke the Bank at Monte Carlo (Fox, 1935)
A Tale of Two Cities (MGM, 1935)
Under Two Flags (20th, 1936)
Lost Horizon (Col., 1937)
The Prisoner of Zenda (UA, 1937)
If I Were King (Par., 1938)
The Light That Failed (Par., 1939)
Lucky Partners (RKO, 1940)
My Life with Caroline (RKO, 1941)
The Talk of the Town (Col., 1942)
Random Harvest (MGM, 1942)

Ronald Colman plays a soldier who is an amnesia victim hospitalized for shell shock. Greer Garson is the lady who helps him to recover in *Random Harvest* (MGM, 1942).

Kismet (MGM, 1944)
The Late George Apley (20th, 1947)
A Double Life (Univ., 1948)
Champagne for Caesar (UA, 1950)
Around the World in 80 Days (UA, 1956)
The Story of Mankind (WB, 1957)

Gary Cooper
(1901–1961)

Cooper was born in Helena, Montana, and received his elementary education in England. After graduating from Grinnell College in Iowa, he went to California hoping to work on a newspaper as a cartoonist. Failing to get the employment he wanted, he worked at odd jobs and began playing extra roles in cowboy movies of the silent era. He was cast in Goldwyn's *The Winning of Barbara Worth* with Ronald Colman and Vilma Banky. That part paved the way to better roles and a contract with Paramount. There he made films with Clara Bow, Fay Wray, Colleen Moore, Nancy Carroll and Lupe Velez. His first sound film, *The Virginian*, was a box office hit and made him a star. From 1936 to 1957 he was a top box office draw, appearing with Marlene Dietrich, Tallulah Bankhead, Jean Arthur, Barbara Stanwyck, Carole Lombard, Loretta Young and other top female stars.

He won two Oscars for his roles in *Sergeant York* and *High Noon*. Just before his death in 1961 he received a special Academy Award for his many memorable screen performances and the international recognition which he was an individual had gained for the motion picture industry.

Gary Cooper Sound Films (1929–1961)

The Virginian (Par., 1929)
Only the Brave (Par., 1930)
Paramount on Parade (Par., 1930)
The Texan (Par., 1930)
Seven Days Leave (Par., 1930)
A Man from Wyoming (Par., 1930)
The Spoilers (Par., 1930)
Morocco (Par., 1930)
Fighting Caravans (Par., 1931)
City Streets (Par., 1931)
I Take This Woman (Par., 1931)
His Woman (Par., 1931)
The Devil and the Deep (Par., 1932)
Make Me a Star (Par., 1932)
If I Had a Million (Par., 1932)
Farewell to Arms (Par., 1932)
Today We Live (MGM, 1933)
One Sunday Afternoon (Par., 1933)
Design for Living (Par., 1933)

Gary Cooper

Gary Cooper in *High Noon* as the marshal of Hadleyville who stands alone against the gunslingers planning to kill him (United Artists, 1952).

Alice in Wonderland (Par., 1933)
Operator 13 (MGM, 1934)
Now and Forever (Par., 1934)
Wedding Night (UA, 1935)
Lives of a Bengal Lancer (Par., 1935)
Peter Ibbetson (Par., 1935)
Desire (Par., 1936)
Mr. Deeds Goes to Town (Col., 1936)
The General Died at Dawn (Par., 1936)
Hollywood Boulevard (Par., 1936)
The Plainsman (Par., 1936)
Souls at Sea (Par., 1937)
Adventures of Marco Polo (UA, 1938)

Bluebeard's Eighth Wife (Par., 1938)
The Cowboy and the Lady (UA, 1938)
Beau Geste (Par., 1939)
The Westerner (UA, 1940)
North West Mounted Police (Par., 1940)
Meet John Doe (WB, 1941)
Sergeant York (WB, 1941)
Ball of Fire (RKO, 1941)
The Pride of the Yankees (RKO, 1942)
For Whom the Bell Tolls (Par., 1943)
The Story of Dr. Wassell (Par., 1944)
Casanova Brown (RKO, 1944)

Along Came Jones (RKO, 1945)
Saratoga Trunk (WB, 1945)
Cloak and Dagger (WB, 1946)
Unconquered (Par., 1947)
Variety Girl (Par., 1947)
Good Sam (RKO, 1948)
The Fountainhead (WB, 1949)
It's a Great Feeling (WB, 1949)
Task Force (WB, 1949)
Bright Leaf (WB, 1950)
Dallas (WB, 1950)
You're in the Navy Now (20th, 1951)
Starlift (WB, 1951)
It's a Big Country (WB, 1951)
Distant Drums (WB, 1951)
High Noon (UA, 1952)
Springfield Rifle (WB, 1952)
Return to Paradise (UA, 1953)
Blowing Wild (WB, 1953)
Garden of Evil (20th, 1954)
Vera Cruz (UA, 1954)
The Court Martial of Billy Mitchell (WB, 1955)
Friendly Persuasion (AA, 1956)
Love in the Afternoon (AA, 1957)
Ten North Frederick (20th, 1958)
Man of the West (UA, 1958)
The Hanging Tree (WB, 1959)
They Came to Cordura (Col., 1959)
The Wreck of the Mary Deare (MGM, 1959)
Alias Jesse James (unbilled guest appearance; UA, 1959)
The Naked Edge (UA, 1961)

Joan Crawford
(1904–1977)

Born Lucille LeSueur in San Antonio, Texas, she worked as a waitress and shopgirl before winning a Charleston contest. She changed her name to Billie Cassin and, after dancing in night clubs in Chicago and Detroit, she was in the chorus of a hit musical. Henry Rapf of MGM discovered her and after a screen test she was signed to a contract. A nationwide contest resulted in her new name, Joan Crawford. In the silent era she appeared with such top stars as Charles Ray, Owen Moore, Tim McCoy, Lon Chaney, John Gilbert and William Haines. She made a successful transition from silent to sound movies and for many years she was one of MGM's brightest stars. After leaving MGM she went to Warner Brothers. At Warner she made *Mildred Pierce* which won her an Oscar in 1945.

Top: Clark Gable is an escaped prisoner from Devil's Island and Joan Crawford is the cafe entertainer who helps him in *Strange Cargo* (MGM, 1940). *Bottom:* Joan Crawford is a successful novelist being romanced by Herbert Marshall, her publisher who is married and a cheat in *When Ladies Meet* (MGM, 1941).

Three of her husbands, Douglas Fairbanks, Jr., Franchot Tone and Phillip Terry, were actors. These marriages ended in divorce. In 1956 she married Alfred Steele, chairman of Pepsi-Cola. She was a board member and publicity executive for the company even after his death. She returned occasionally to make films and wrote two books about herself, *A Portrait of Joan* and *My Way of Life*.

Joan Crawford Sound Films (1929–1970)

Hollywood Revue of 1929 (MGM, 1929)
Untamed (MGM, 1929)
Montana Moon (MGM, 1930)
Our Blushing Brides (MGM, 1930)
Paid (MGM, 1930)
Dance, Fools, Dance (MGM, 1931)
Laughing Sinners (MGM, 1931)
This Modern Age (MGM, 1931)
Possessed (MGM, 1931)
Grand Hotel (MGM, 1932)
Letty Lynton (MGM, 1932)
Today We Live (MGM, 1933)
Dancing Lady (MGM, 1933)
Sadie McKee MGM, 1934)
Chained (MGM, 1934)
Forsaking All Others (MGM, 1934)
No More Ladies (MGM, 1935)
The Gorgeous Hussy (MGM, 1936)
Love on the Run (MGM, 1936)
The Last of Mrs. Cheyney (MGM, 1937)
The Bride Wore Red (MGM, 1937)
Mannequin (MGM, 1938)
The Shining Hour (MGM, 1938)
Ice Follies of 1939, (MGM, 1939)
The Women (MGM, 1939)
Strange Cargo (MGM, 1940)
Susan and God (MGM, 1940)
A Woman's Face (MGM, 1941)

When Ladies Meet (MGM, 1941)
They All Kissed the Bride (Col., 1942)
Reunion in France (MGM, 1942)
Above Suspicion (MGM, 1943)
Hollywood Canteen (WB, 1944)
Mildred Pierce (WB, 1945)
Humoresque (WB, 1946)
Possessed (WB, 1947)
Daisy Kenyon (20th, 1947)
Flamingo Road (WB, 1949)
The Damned Don't Cry (WB, 1950)
Harriet Craig (Col., 1950)
Goodbye, My Fancy (WB, 1951)
This Man Is Dangerous (WB, 1952)
Sudden Fear (RKO, 1952)
Torch Song (MGM, 1953)
Johnny Guitar (Rep., 1954)
Female on the Beach (Univ., 1955)
Queen Bee (Col., 1955)
Autumn Leaves (Col., 1956)
The Best of Everything (20th, 1959)
What Ever Happened to Baby Jane? (WB, 1962)
The Caretakers (UA, 1963)
Strait-Jacket (Col., 1964)
I Saw What You Did (Univ., 1965)
Berserk! (Col., 1967)
Trog (WB, 1970)

Bing Crosby
(1904–1977)

Born in Tacoma, Washington, he attended Gonzaga University and worked as a singer and drummer in a combo. After joining Paul Whiteman's band as one of the Rhythm Boys, he made independent musical shorts and recordings. These led to a contract with Paramount. At that studio he became a top box office draw. he also worked for MGM, Universal, RKO and 20th–Century in top musical hits. At his home studio he teamed with Bob Hope and Dorothy Lamour in the highly successful "Road" pictures. His records were best sellers and he became a top performer on radio. His first marriage to Dixie Lee produced four sons. Five years after her death he married Kathryn Grant. They had two sons and a daughter.

Crosby won an Academy Award for his portrayal of a priest in *Going My Way* in 1944. He appeared regularly on television and his personal appearances received glowing reviews. He died in Spain in 1977.

Bing Crosby Feature Films (1930–1974)

King of Jazz (Univ., 1930)
The Big Broadcast (Par., 1932)
College Humor (Par., 1933)
Too Much Harmony (Par., 1933)
Going Hollywood (MGM, 1933)
We're Not Dressing (Par., 1934)
She Loves Me Not (Par., 1934)
Mississippi (Par., 1935)
Two for Tonight (Par., 1935)
Big Broadcast of 1936 (Par., 1935)
Anything Goes (Par., 1936)
Rhythm on the Range (Par., 1936)
Pennies from Heaven (Par., 1936)
Waikiki Wedding (Par., 1937)
Double or Nothing (Par., 1937)
Dr. Rhythm (Par., 1938)
Sing You Sinners (Par., 1938)

Paris Honeymoon (Par., 1939)
East Side of Heaven (Univ., 1939)
The Star Maker (Par., 1939)
Road to Singapore (Par., 1940)
If I Had My Way (Univ., 1940)
Rhythm on the River (Par., 1940)
Road to Zanzibar (Par., 1941)
Birth of the Blues (Par., 1941)
My Favorite Blonde (Par., 1942)
Road to Morocco (Par., 1942)
Star Spangled Rhythm (Par., 1942)
Dixie (Par., 1943)
Going My Way (Par., 1944)
The Princess and the Pirate (unbilled guest appearance; RKO, 1944)

Bing Crosby *(left)* **and Bob Hope were paired for the first time in** *The Road to Singapore.* **It was Paramount's biggest-grossing picture in 1940 and led to other "Road" pictures (Paramount, 1940).**

Here Come the Waves (Par., 1945)
Duffy's Tavern (Par., 1945)
Road to Utopia (Par., 1945)
Out of This World (voice only; Par., 1945)
The Bells of St. Mary's (RKO, 1945)
Blue Skies (Par., 1946)
Variety Girl (Par., 1947)
Welcome Stranger (Par., 1947)
My Favorite Brunette (unbilled guest appearance; Par., 1947)
Road to Rio (Par., 1947)
The Emperor Waltz (Par., 1948)
A Connecticut Yankee in King Arthur's Court (Par., 1949)
The Adventures of Ichabod and

Mr. Toad (voice only; RKO, 1949)
Top o' the Morning (Par., 1949)
Riding High (Par., 1950)
Mr. Music (Par., 1950)
Here Comes the Groom (Par., 1951)
The Greatest Show on Earth (unbilled guest appearance; Par., 1952)
Just for You (Par., 1952)
Son of Paleface (unbilled guest appearance; Par., 1952)
Road to Bali (Par., 1952)
Scared Stiff (unbilled guest appearance; Par., 1953)
Little Boy Lost (Par., 1953)
White Christmas (Par., 1954)

Top: Bing Crosby and Joan Caulfield in *Blue Skies*. Irving Berlin songs including "Blue Skies," "Puttin' on the Ritz" and "White Christmas" made this film a hit musical (Paramount, 1946). *Bottom:* Bing Crosby is a young, easygoing priest who is sent to St. Dominick's Church. Barry Fitzgerald, the older priest who has been there for 45 years, is more traditional but all comes out well in *Going My Way* (Paramount, 1944).

The Country Girl (Par., 1954)
Anything Goes (Par., 1956)
High Society (MGM, 1956)
Man on Fire (MGM, 1957)
Say One for Me (20th, 1959)
Alias Jesse James (unbilled
   guest appearance; UA, 1959)
High Time (20th, 1960)
Pepe (Col., 1960)

Road to Hong Kong (UA,
   1962)
Robin and the 7 Hoods (WB,
   1964)
Bing Crosby's Cinerama Adventures (Cinerama, 1966)
Stagecoach (20th, 1966)
That's Entertainment (on-screen
   narrator; MGM, 1974)

Marion Davies
(1897–1961)

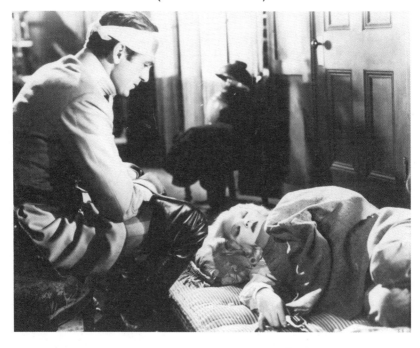

Marion Davies is an actress during the Civil War who becomes a Union spy behind the Confederate lines and Gary Cooper is the Southern officer in *Operator 13* **(MGM, 1934).**

Marion Davies was born in Brooklyn and made her Broadway debut in a chorus line at the age of sixteen. After making a silent film directed by her brother-in-law, she came to the attention of newspaper

Marion Davies is a French teacher and Bing Crosby is a crooner who end up *Going Hollywood* and becoming overnight sensations in this lighthearted musical (MGM, 1933).

magnate William Randolph Hearst. He took a great interest in her career and managed it for many years. He formed Cosmopolitan Pictures to produce her films under his supervision, later releasing them first through Paramount and then MGM. With the passing of silent films, she made a successful transition to sound. She was a talented light comedienne but Hearst cast her in types which were not her forte. After a disagreement with MGM executives Hearst moved his film company to

Marion Davies plays a Baltimore girl who becomes involved with Napoleon's
brother in *Hearts Divided*. Henry Stephenson is her father and Clara Blandick
(far right) plays her aunt (Warner Bros., 1936).

Warner Brothers. Her film career ended in 1937 when the Hearst empire was in great financial stress. After Hearst's death in 1951, she married and was a successful and wealthy business woman.

Marion Davies Sound Films (1929–1937)

Marianne (MGM, 1929)
Hollywood Revue of 1929
  (MGM, 1929)
Not So Dumb (MGM, 1930)
Floradora Girl (MGM, 1930)
Bachelor Father (MGM, 1931)
It's a Wise Child (MGM, 1931)
Five and Ten (MGM, 1931)
Polly of the Circus (MGM,

  1932)
Peg o' My Heart (MGM, 1933)
Going Hollywood (MGM, 1933)
Operator 13 (MGM, 1934)
Page Miss Glory (WB, 1935)
Hearts Divided (WB, 1936)
Cain and Mabel (WB, 1936)
Ever Since Eve (WB, 1937

James Dean
(1931–1955)

Sal Mineo *(left)*, **James Dean and Natalie Wood star in** *Rebel Without a Cause,*
a powerful study of juvenile violence in which each are seeking identity and
love (Warner Bros., 1955).

James Dean was born in Marion, Indiana, and moved to Los
Angeles at the age of five. After his mother's death three years later he
returned to the midwest where he was raised by an aunt and uncle.
After graduating from high school he went back to California and attended Santa Monica Junior College and UCLA. He began acting with
James Whitmore's little theatre group, appeared in TV commercials
and got bit roles in several films. In 1953 he went to New York where
he observed classes at Actors Studio, played bit roles in TV dramas and
made his Broadway debut in the play *See the Jaguar.* He won a Tony
award in 1954 for his performance in *The Immoralist,* a play adapted
from Andre Gide's novel of the same name. After a successful screen

As Cal, James Dean is troubled and troublesome, challenging authority and believing he is not loved by his father in *East of Eden.* Julie Harris learns to deal with Cal's self-destruction (Warner Bros., 1955).

test he signed a contract with Warner Brothers. Two pictures and a year later he was a top Hollywood star. His career culminated with a starring role in the memorable *Giant.* It was released after his tragic death in a car crash at the age of twenty-four in Paso Robles, California.

James Dean Feature Films (1951–1956)

Sailor Beware (Par., 1951)
Fixed Bayonets (20th, 1951)
Has Anybody Seen My Gal(Univ., 1952)

East of Eden (WB, 1955)
Rebel Without a Cause (WB, 1955)
Giant (WB, 1956)

Opposite: James Dean, as Jett Rink in *Giant,* escaped the type-casting of a young rebel to play a role which revealed his great talent as an actor (Warner Bros., 1956).

Melvyn Douglas
(1901–1981)

Melvyn Douglas was born in Mason, Georgia, and became a leading Broadway actor. Going to Hollywood in 1931 in the screen version of the hit play *Tonight or Never*, he became a suave and polished leading man in films. He married Helen Gahagan and they had three children—Gregory, Peter and Mary. In World War II he served in the navy in the China-Burma-India area. He appeared opposite such stars as Gloria Swanson, Claudette Colbert, Sylvia Sidney, Barbara Stanwyck, Irene Dunne, Joan Crawford, and Greta Garbo. He returned to the New York stage as Paul Muni's replacement in *Inherit the Wind*. In his next play, *The Best Man*, he won the honored Tony award for his performance. Other hit plays followed with *Spofford* (in which he toured the U.S.) and *I Never Sang for My Father*. He repeated his role in the latter in a film version. He made several important television appearances and won an Emmy for his performance in *Do Not Go Gentle into That Good Night*. He won two Oscars for best supporting actor in *Hud* and *Being There*. In 1981, at the age of eighty, he died in New York after a brief illness.

Melvyn Douglas Film Credits (1931–1981)

Tonight or Never (UA, 1931)
Prestige (RKO, 1932)
The Wiser Sex (Par., 1932)
Broken Wing (Par., 1932)
As You Desire Me (MGM, 1932)
The Old Dark House (Univ., 1932)
Nagana (Univ., 1933)
The Vampire Bat (Majestic, 1933)
Counsellor-at-Law (Univ., 1933)
Woman in the Dark (RKO, 1934)
Dangerous Corner (RKO, 1934)
People's Enemy (RKO, 1935)

She Married Her Boss (Col., 1935)
Mary Burns—Fugitive (Par., 1935)
Annie Oakley (RKO, 1935)
The Lone Wolf Returns (Col., 1936)
And So They Were Married (Col., 1936)
The Gorgeous Hussy (MGM, 1936)
Theodora Goes Wild (Col., 1936)
Women of Glamour (Col., 1937)
Captains Courageous (MGM, 1937)

Top: Greta Garbo as *Ninotchka* with Melvyn Douglas poked fun at the Soviets and Stalin-dominated Russia in this delightful comedy under the gifted direction of Ernst Lubitsch (MGM, 1939). *Bottom:* Joan Crawford is a tough businesswoman devoted to running a trucking firm which she inherited. She attends a truckers' dance with Mary Treen *(left)*, Allen Jenkins and Melvyn Douglas and learns something about compassion in *They All Kissed the Bride* (Col., 1942).

I Met Him in Paris (Par., 1937)
Angel (Par., 1937)
I'll Take Romance (Col., 1937)
There's Always a Woman (Col., 1938)
Arsene Lupin Returns (MGM, 1938)
The Toy Wife (MGM, 1938)
Fast Company (MGM, 1938)
The Shining Hour (MGM, 1938)
There's That Woman Again (Col., 1938)
Tell No Tales (MGM, 1939)
Good Girls Go to Paris (Col., 1939)
The Amazing Mr. Williams (Col., 1939)
Ninotchka (MGM, 1939)
Too Many Husbands (Col., 1940)
He Stayed for Breakfast (Col., 1940)
Third Finger—Left Hand (MGM, 1940)
This Thing Called Love (Col., 1941)
That Uncertain Feeling (Col., 1941)
A Woman's Face (MGM, 1941)
Our Wife (Col., 1941)
Two-Faced Woman (MGM, 1941)
They All Kissed the Bride (Col., 1942)
Three Hearts for Julia (MGM, 1943)
The Sea of Grass (MGM, 1947)
The Guilt of Janet Ames (Col., 1947)
Mr. Blandings Builds His Dream House (RKO, 1948)
My Own True Love (Par., 1948)
A Woman's Secret (RKO, 1949)
The Great Sinner (MGM, 1949)
My Forbidden Past (RKO, 1951)
On the Loose (RKO, 1951)
Billy Budd (AA, 1962)
Hud (Par., 1963)
Advance to the Rear (MGM, 1964)
The Americanization of Emily (MGM, 1964)
Rapture (International Classics, 1965)
Hotel (WB, 1967)
I Never Sang for My Father (Col., 1970)
One Is a Lonely Number (MGM, 1972)
The Candidate (WB, 1972)
Hunters Are for Killing (Univ., 1974)
The Tenant (Par., 1976)
Twilight's Last Gleaming (AA, 1977)
The Seduction of Joe Tynan (Univ., 1979)
The Challenging (AIP, 1979)
Being There (UA, 1979)
Tell Me a Riddle (AIP, 1980)
Gas (Par., 1981)
French Kiss (Foreign, 1981)
Ghost Story (Univ., 1981)

Marie Dressler
(1869–1934)

Marie Dressler (christened Leila Koerber), the daughter of a music teacher, was born in Canada. At fourteen she left home, took the name

As the captain of a tugboat Marie Dressler, with Frankie Darro as her young son, refuses to leave the tugboat even when life hands them some unkind blows in *Tugboat Annie* (MGM, 1933).

Marie Dressler, and worked in theatrical touring companies. She received further experience with the George Baker Opera Company and appeared with Eddie Foy, Maurice Barrymore and Lillian Russell on Broadway. She then toured with Joe Weber, formerly of the great vaudeville team of Weber and Fields. Stardom came to her when she played the lead in *Tillie's Nightmare* in which she sang *Heaven Will Protect the Working Girl*. She was signed by Mack Sennett and made films for him. The most successful was *Tillie Punctured Romance* with Charlie Chaplin. During World War I she sold war bonds and entertained the

Marie Dressler *(left)* and Polly Moran were teamed for the fourth and last time in *Prosperity.* The pair gave their all to the roles in this laugh-loaded escape entertainment. (MGM, 1932).

troops. Screenwriter Frances Marion persuaded her to return to films in 1927. This led to a contract with MGM.

She won an Academy Award in 1931 for *Min and Bill* opposite Wallace Beery. For four years she was the top box-office star in the United States. She penned her autobiography entitled *The Life of an Ugly Duckling.*

Marie Dressler Sound Film Credits (1929–1933)

Hollywood Revue of 1929 (MGM, 1929)

The Vagabond Lover (RKO, 1929)

Chasing Rainbows (MGM, 1930)
The Girl Said No (MGM, 1930)
Anna Christie, (MGM, 1930)
One Romantic Night (UA, 1930)
Caught Short (MGM, 1930)
Let Us Be Gay (MGM, 1930)
Min and Bill (MGM, 1930)

Reducing (MGM, 1931)
Politics (MGM, 1931)
Emma (MGM, 1932)
Prosperity (MGM, 1932)
Dinner at Eight (MGM, 1933)
Christopher Beam (MGM, 1933)
Tugboat Annie (MGM, 1933)

Nelson Eddy
(1901–1967)

In *I Married an Angel,* Nelson Eddy *(left)* stars as a bored playboy who runs a bank and escapes into a fantasy world. Ludwig Stossel is the janitor (MGM, 1942).

Nelson Eddy was born in Providence, Rhode Island. In his teens he moved to Philadelphia and worked as a shipping clerk. He then became a newspaper reporter. He appeared in amateur musicals and won a competition to sing with the Philadelphia Civic Opera. After

Maytime featured the third teaming of Nelson Eddy and Jeanette MacDonald and was the favorite of their fans. They had much to do, many songs to sing, and proved they had more depth as actors than had been generally acknowledged (MGM, 1937).

making a name for himself in opera, he turned to concerts and radio work. He was signed by MGM but appeared only briefly in his first three films.

Louis B. Mayer was responsible for casting Eddy opposite Jeanette McDonald in *Naughty Marietta*, a blockbuster at the box office. As a team under producer Hunt Stromberg, Eddy and McDonald became known as *America's Singing Sweethearts* and sang together in nine great Hollywood musicals from 1935 to 1942. After leaving MGM, Eddy appeared in other musicals but not as successfully. He made records, appeared in concerts, and did nightclub work. He died on stage in a nightclub on Miami Beach.

Nelson Eddy Film Credits (1933–1947)

Broadway to Hollywood (MGM, 1933)
Dancing Lady (MGM, 1933)
Student Tour (MGM, 1934)
Naughty Marietta (MGM, 1935)
Rose Marie (MGM, 1936)
Maytime (MGM, 1937)
Rosalie (MGM, 1937)
Girl of the Golden West (MGM, 1938)
Sweethearts (MGM, 1938)
Let Freedom Ring (MGM, 1939)
Balalaika (MGM, 1939)

New Moon (MGM, 1940)
Bitter Sweet (MGM, 1940)
The Chocolate Soldier (MGM, 1941)
I Married An Angel (MGM, 1942)
The Phantom of the Opera (Univ., 1943)
Knickerbocker Holiday (UA, 1944)
Make Mine Music (voices only; RKO, 1946)
Northwest Outpost (Rep., 1947)

W.C. Fields
(1879–1946)

At the age of eleven Fields ran away from his parents who were Cockney immigrants living a hand-to-mouth existence in Philadelphia. To survive Fields did odd jobs. He learned to be a juggler and his first job was at an amusement park. After some years of experience, he prospered and became a headliner in vaudeville, playing Europe, Africa and Australia. He returned to star on Broadway, worked for Ziegfeld and appeared in *George White's Scandals*. His first silent short was *Pool Sharks,* made in 1915. A decade later Paramount filmed *Sally of the Sawdust,* the movie version of *Poppy,* in which Fields had been a hit as the male lead. In *Sally,* directed by D.W. Griffith, he supported Carol Dempster and Alfred Lunt. His contract with Paramount paid him for his acting roles and an additional amount for writing his own material.

He made a successful transition to sound films and remained under contract to Paramount. He was loaned out only twice, for *Her Majesty*

Top: If I Had a Million is made of many segments linked together by a multi-millionaire who leaves his money to total strangers, including W.C. Fields (Paramount, 1932). *Bottom:* W.C. Fields coos *My Little Chickadee* to Mae West in this western satire. She asks him to "Come up and see me sometime" (Universal, 1940).

Love at Warners opposite Marilyn Miller and for *David Copperfield* with an all-star cast at MGM. He received glowing reviews for both. Later he moved to Universal Studios and made films with Charley McCarthy, Edgar Bergen and Mae West. He also starred in radio. A film biography of his life starred Rod Steiger as Fields.

W.C. Fields Sound Film Credits (1931–1944)

Her Majesty Love (WB, 1931)
Million Dollar Legs (Par., 1932)
If I Had a Million (Par., 1932)
International House (Par., 1933)
Tillie and Gus (Par., 1933)
Alice in Wonderland (Par., 1933)
Six of a Kind (Par., 1934)
You're Telling Me (Par., 1934)
Old Fashioned Way (Par., 1934)
Mrs. Wiggs of the Cabbage Patch (Par., 1934)
It's a Gift (Par., 1934)
David Copperfield (MGM, 1935)
Mississippi (Par., 1935)
The Man on the Flying Trapeze (Par., 1935)
Poppy (Par., 1936)
Big Broadcast of 1938 (Par., 1938)
You Can't Cheat an Honest Man (Univ., 1939)
My Little Chickadee (Univ., 1940)
The Bank Dick (Univ., 1940)
Never Give a Sucker an Even Break (Univ., 1941)
Follow the Boys (Univ., 1944)
Song of the Open Road (UA, 1944)
Sensations of 1945 (UA, 1944)

Errol Flynn
(1909–1959)

Errol Flynn was born in Hobart, Tasmania, and educated in Australia and England. He had little interest in schooling and at the age of sixteen he was a shipping clerk for a Sydney company. From there he went to New Guinea to search for gold and also managed a plantation. While there he made a documentary film in which he played Fletcher Christian. He then went to England and acted with the Northhampton Repertory Company. Some of their productions moved to London for further exposure. He was seen there by a Warner Brothers' talent scout and offered a contract. He came to the United States and appeared in a few films before his big chance in *Captain Blood,* a role

Errol Flynn *(right)* **as the Earl of Essex returns triumphantly to London after conquering the Spanish and is greeted by Frances Bacon, played by Donald Crisp in** *Private Lives of Elizabeth and Essez* **(Warner Bros., 1939).**

which other actors had turned down. Overnight he became a Hollywood star. He remained a top box office draw for many years under Warner Brothers until they gave him inferior parts. He went to Europe, made some poor films, and his career went into a slump. Later he returned to Hollywood and got excellent reviews for 20th–Century. He was married three times, first to Lili Damita, then to Nora Eddington, and finally to Patricia Wymore. He died of a heart attack at the age of fifty in Vancouver, Canada.

Errol Flynn Film Credits (1933–1959)

In the Wake of the Bounty
(Australian, 1933)
Murder in Monte Carlo (WB,
1935)

The Case of the Curious Bride
(WB, 1935)
Don't Bet on Blondes (WB,
1935)

Captain Blood made stars of Errol Flynn and Olivia de Havilland. Both had limited screen experience but shined under the direction of Michael Curtiz (Warner Bros., 1935).

Captain Blood (WB, 1935)
I Found Stella Parish (WB, 1935)
The Charge of the Light Brigade (WB, 1936)
Green Light (WB, 1937)
The Prince and the Pauper (WB, 1937)
Another Dawn (WB, 1937)
The Perfect Specimen (WB, 1937)
The Adventure of Robin Hood (WB, 1938)
Four's a Crowd (WB, 1938)
The Sisters (WB, 1938)
The Dawn Patrol (WB, 1938)
Dodge City (WB, 1939)
The Private Lives of Elizabeth and Essex (WB, 1939)
Virginia City (WB, 1940)
The Sea Hawk (WB, 1940)
Santa Fe Trail (WB, 1940)
Footsteps in the Dark (WB, 1941)

Dive Bomber (WB, 1941)
They Died with Their Boots On
   (WB, 1941)
Desperate Journey (WB, 1942)
Gentleman Jim (WB, 1942)
Edge of Darkness (WB, 1943)
Thank Your Lucky Stars (WB,
   1943)
Uncertain Glory (WB, 1944)
Objective Burma (WB, 1945)
San Antonio (WB, 1945)
Never Say Goodbye (WB, 1946)
Cry Wolf (WB, 1947)
Escape Me Never (WB, 1947)
Silver River (WB, 1948)
The Adventures of Don Juan
   (WB, 1948)
That Forsyte Woman (MGM,
   1949)
Hello God (William Marshall,
   1950)
Montana (WB, 1950)

Rocky Mountain (WB, 1950)
Kim (MGM, 1950)
The Adventures of Captain Fa-
   bian (Rep., 1951)
Mara Maru (WB, 1952)
Against All Flags (Univ., 1952)
The Master of Ballantrae (WB,
   1953)
Crossed Swords (UA, 1953)
Lilacs in the Spring (Rep., 1955)
The Warriors (AA, 1955)
King's Rhapsody (British Lion,
   1955)
The Big Boodle (UA, 1957)
Istanbul (Univ., 1957)
The Sun Also Rises (20th, 1957)
Too Much, Too Soon (WB,
   1958)
The Roots of Heaven (20th,
   1958)
Cuban Rebel Girls (Joseph
   Brenner Associates, 1959)

Henry Fonda
(1905–1982)

Henry Fonda was born in Grand Island, Nebraska, and raised in Omaha where his father owned a printing company. After dropping out of college he became interested in the theatre and joined a little theatre group. He did some design as well as acting. In 1928 Fonda joined the Provincetown Players on Cape Cod. This led to his involvement with University Players summer theatre where he met Margaret Sullavan (to whom he was married briefly), James Stewart and Joshua Logan. His first big break was in Leonard Sillman's *New Faces* with Imogene Coca in 1934. Hollywood producer Walter Wanger signed him to a contract and he appeared opposite Janet Gaynor in his first film. It was the beginning of a highly successful movie career. In 1942 he joined the navy and served in the central Pacific and the Marianas where he received the Bronze Star and a presidential citation. After his discharge in 1945, he returned briefly to the screen and then spent seven years on the New

York stage. He starred in *Mister Roberts, Point of No Return* and *The Caine Mutiny.* He won these distinguished awards: The American Film Institute's Life Achievement Award (1978), an honorary Oscar (1981), and an Oscar for best actor opposite Katharine Hepburn in *On Golden Pond* (1981). He died of heart failure at 77. Surviving are his wife Shirlee, daughter Jane, son Peter and an adopted daughter Amy.

Henry Fonda Film Credits (1935–1981)

The Farmer Takes a Wife (Fox, 1935)

Way Down East (Fox, 1935)

I Dream Too Much (RKO, 1935)

Trail of the Lonesome Pine (Par., 1936)

The Moon's Our Home (Par., 1936)

Spendthrift (Par., 1936)

Wings of the Morning (20th, 1937)

You Only Live Once (UA, 1937)

Slim (WB, 1937)

That Certain Woman (WB, 1937)

I Met My Love Again (UA, 1938)

Jezebel (WB, 1938)

Blockade (UA, 1938)

Spawn of the North (Par., 1938)

The Mad Miss Manton (RKO, 1938)

Jesse James (20th, 1939)

Let Us Live (Col., 1939)

Story of Alexander Graham Ball (20th, 1939)

Young Mr. Lincoln (20th, 1939)

Drums Along the Mohawk (20th, 1939)

The Grapes of Wrath (20th, 1940)

Lillian Russell (20th, 1940)

The Return of Frank James (20th, 1940)

Chad Hanna (20th, 1940)

The Lady Eve (Par., 1941)

Wild Geese Calling (20th, 1941)

You Belong to Me (Col., 1941)

The Male Animal (WB, 1942)

Rings on Her Fingers (20th, 1942)

The Magnificent Dope (20th, 1942)

Tales of Manhattan (20th, 1942)

The Big Street (RKO, 1942)

The Immortal Sergeant (20th, 1943)

The Ox-Bow Incident (20th, 1943)

My Darling Clementine (20th, 1946)

The Long Night (RKO, 1947)

The Fugitive (RKO, 1947)

Daisy Kenyon (20th, 1947)

On Our Merry Way (UA, 1948)

Fort Apache (RKO, 1948)

Jigsaw (UA, 1949)

Mister Roberts (WB, 1955)

War and Peace (Par., 1956)

The Wrong Man (WB, 1957)

12 Angry Men (UA, 1957)

The Star (Par., 1957)

Stage Struck (BV, 1958)

Warlock (20th, 1959)

The Man Who Understood Women (20th, 1959)

Advise and Consent (Col., 1962)

The Longest Day (20th, 1962)

How the West Was Won (20th, 1963)

Spencer's Mountain (WB, 1963)

Top: James Stewart defends his land against a bunch of hoodlums (*left to right,* James Best, Gary Lockwood, Henry Fonda, Jack Elam and Morgan Woodward) in *Firecreek* (Warner Bros.-7 Arts, 1968). *Bottom:* Robert Ryan as General Grey tries to convince Henry Fonda that the German tanks will be used elsewhere in *Battle of the Bulge* (Warner Bros., 1959).

On Golden Pond tells of an elderly couple (Henry Fonda and Katharine Hepburn) who return for one last holiday at their summer cottage (Universal, 1981).

The Best Man (UA, 1964)
Fail Safe (Col., 1964)
Sex and the Single Girl (WB, 1964)
The Rounders (MGM, 1965)
In Harm's Way (Par., 1965)
The Battle of the Bulge (WB, 1965)
The Dirty Game (AIP, 1966)
A Big Hand for the Little Lady (WB, 1966)
Welcome to Hard Times (MGM, 1967)
Firecreek (WB-7 Arts, 1968)
Madigan (Univ., 1968)
Yours, Mine and Ours (UA, 1968)
Boston Strangler (20th, 1968)

Once Upon a Time in the West (Par., 1969)
Cheyenne Social Club (NGP, 1970)
There Was a Crooked Man (WB, 1970)
Too Late the Hero (Cinerama, 1970)
Sometimes a Great Notion (Univ., 1971)
The Sergeant (French-W. German, 1978)
My Name Is Nobody (Titanus, 1973)
Ash Wednesday (Par., 1973)
Mussolini (Par., 1974)
Midway (Univ., 1976)
Rollercoaster (Univ., 1977)

Tentacles (20th, 1977)
Last of the Cowboys (Indepen-
   dent, 1977)
The Swami (WB, 1978)
Meteor (AIP, 1978)

Fedora (cameo; Rialto Films,
   1978)
City on Fire (Astral Films,
   1979)
On Golden Pond (Univ., 1981)

Kay Francis
(1903–1968)

Kay Francis *(center)* **stars as a welfare worker for the San Francisco Traveler's Aid. She becomes involved with workers on the Golden Gate Bridge in** *Stranded* **(Warner Bros., 1935).**

Kay Francis was born in Oklahoma City where her father was a businessman and her mother an actress. After a convent education, she worked as a secretary and a real estate agent. She became interested in the theatre and did stock work, which led her to Broadway. She was an understudy for Katherine Cornell and played opposite Basil Sydney and Walter Huston before being signed by Paramount. At that studio she

As a glamourous actress in *I Found Stella Parish* Kay Francis tries to hide her unsavory past from her daughter, only to be exposed by the press (Warner Bros., 1935).

gained international stardom and was loaned to MGM and RKO. She and Ruth Chatterton both left Paramount and went to Warner Brothers. At Warner Brothers she made the classic *One Way Passage* with William Powell.

She was lent to Samuel Goldwyn for *Cyrano* in which she played opposite Ronald Colman because her other loan-out to the Paramount director Ernst Lubitish in *Trouble in Paradise* went over schedule. Her subsequent films at Warner Brothers were weak and she eventually left the studio. She worked at other studios and co-produced some of her last films. During World War II she toured overseas for the U.S.O. with Martha Raye, Carole Landis and Mitzi Mayfair. She returned to Broadway in 1946 in the hit play *State of the Union* and then played it on the road. Thereafter she played in stock until her retirement.

She died of cancer and left a two million dollar estate to charities.

Kay Francis Feature Films (1929–1946)

Gentlemen of the Press (Par., 1929)
The Cocoanuts (Par., 1929)
Dangerous Curves (Par., 1929)
Illusion (Par., 1929)
The Marriage Playground (Par., 1929)
Behind the Makeup (Par., 1930)
The Street of Chance (Par., 1930)
Paramount on Parade (Par., 1930)
A Notorious Affair (WB, 1930)
Raffles (UA, 1930)
For the Defense (Par, 1930)
Let's Go Native (Par., 1930)
The Virtuous Sin (Par., 1930)
Passion Flower (MGM, 1930)
Scandal Sheet (Par., 1931)
Ladies' Man (Par., 1931)
The Vice Squad (Par., 1931)
Transgression (RKO, 1931)
Guilty Hands (MGM, 1931)
24 Hours (Par., 1931)
Girls About Town (Par., 1931)
The False Madonna (Par., 1932)
Strangers in Love (Par., 1943)
Man Wanted (WB, 1932)
Street of Women (WB, 1932)
Jewel Robbery (WB, 1932)
One Way Passage (WB, 1932)
Trouble in Paradise (Par., 1932)
Cynara (UA, 1932)
The Keyhole (WB, 1933)
Storm at Daybreak (MGM, 1933)
Mary Stevens, M.D. (WB, 1933)
I Loved a Woman (WB, 1933)
House on 56th Street (WB, 1933)
Mandalay (WB, 1934)

Wonder Bar (WB, 1934)
Doctor Monica (WB, 1934)
British Agent (WB, 1934)
Stranded (WB, 1935)
The Goose and the Gander (WB, 1935)
I Found Stella Parish (WB, 1935)
The White Angel (WB, 1936)
Give Me Your Heart (WB, 1936)
Stolen Holiday (WB, 1937)
Confession (WB, 1937)
Another Dawn (WB, 1937)
First Lady (WB, 1937)
Women Are Like That (WB, 1938)
My Bill (WB, 1938)
Secrets of an Actress (WB, 1938)
Comet Over Broadway (WB, 1938)
King of the Underworld (WB, 1939)
Women in the Wind (WB, 1939)
In Name Only (RKO, 1939)
It's a Date (Univ., 1940)
Little Men (RKO, 1940)
When the Daltons Rode (Univ., 1940)
Play Girl (RKO, 1940)
The Man Who Lost Himself (Univ., 1941)
Charley's Aunt (20th, 1941)
The Feminine Touch (MGM, 1941)
Always in My Heart (WB, 1942)
Between Us Girls (Univ., 1942)
Four Jills in a Jeep (20th, 1944)
Divorce (Mon., 1945)
Allotment Wives (Mon., 1945)
Wife Wanted (Mon., 1946)

Clark Gable
(1901–1960)

Gable left school in Ohio to work in a tire factory. In the evenings he did volunteer work backstage in amateur productions and graduated to bit parts. He moved from Ohio to the Oklahoma oil fields where he worked as a driller alongside his father. At 21 he joined a traveling theatre group which went bankrupt. He ended up in Oregon where he became a lunberjack for a short time. He joined another traveling stock company and then went to Hollywood where he obtained work as an extra in silent films. Dissatisfied, he returned to the theatre, did stock work, and made his Broadway debut in 1928. He then played opposite Alice Brady in

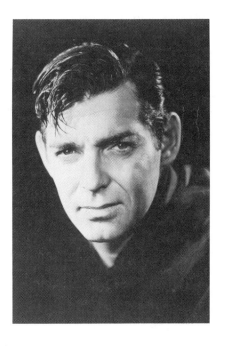

Clark Gable

the hit play *Love, Honor and Obey*. He was signed to play the lead in *The Last Mile* in Los Angeles. While there his friend, Lionel Barrymore, got a screen test for him at MGM but he was not signed. A role in a William Boyd western was the turning point. MGM signed him to a contract and developed him into one of their top stars.

His third wife was actress Carole Lombard, who was killed in a plane crash. He was served in the Air Force during World War II and was decorated for his service in Germany. He was then married briefly to Lady Sylvia Ashley and continued a successful film career. Later he became a free-lancer. With his last wife, Kay Spreckels, he had one son, John Clark, who was born shortly after he died of a heart attack in 1960.

He won one Academy Award opposite Claudette Colbert while on loan to Columbia in Frank Capra's *It Happened One Night*.

Clark Gable Sound Feature Films (1931–1961)

The Painted Desert (Pathé, 1931)
The Easiest Way (MGM, 1931)
Dance Fools Dance (MGM, 1931)
The Secret Six (MGM, 1931)
Laughing Sinners (MGM, 1931)
A Free Soul (MGM, 1931)
Night Nurse (WB, 1931)
Sporting Blood (MGM, 1931)
Susan Lennox—Her Fall and Rise (MGM, 1931)
Possessed (MGM, 1931)
Hell Divers (MGM, 1931)
Polly of the Circus (MGM, 1932)
Strange Interlude (MGM, 1932)
Red Dust (MGM, 1932)
No Man of Her Own (Par., 1932)
The White Sister (MGM, 1933)
Hold Your Man (MGM, 1933)
Night Flight (MGM, 1933)
Dancing Lady (MGM, 1933)
It Happened One Night (Col., 1934)
Men in White (MGM, 1934)
Manhattan Melodrama (MGM, 1934)
Chained (MGM, 1934)
Forsaking All Others (MGM, 1934)
After Office Hours (MGM, 1935)
Call of the Wild (UA, 1935)
China Seas (MGM, 1935)
Mutiny on the Bounty (MGM, 1935)
Wife vs. Secretary (MGM, 1936)
San Francisco (MGM, 1936)
Cain and Mabel (WB, 1936)
Love on the Run (MGM, 1936)

Parnell (MGM, 1937)
Saratoga (MGM, 1937)
Test Pilot (MGM, 1938)
Too Hot to Handle (MGM, 1938)
Idiot's Delight (MGM, 1939)
Gone with the Wind (MGM, 1939)
Strange Cargo (MGM, 1940)
They Met in Bombay (MGM, 1941)
Honky Tonk (MGM, 1941)
Somewhere I'll Find You (MGM, 1942)
Adventure (MGM, 1945)
The Hucksters (MGM, 1947)
Homecoming (MGM, 1948)
Command Decision (MGM, 1948)
Any Number Can Play (MGM, 1949)
Key to the City (MGM, 1950)
To Please a Lady (MGM, 1950)
Across the Wide Missouri (MGM, 1951)
Callaway Went Thataway (MGM, 1951)
Lone Star (MGM, 1952)
Never Let Me Go (MGM, 1953)
Mogambo (MGM, 1953)
Betrayed (MGM, 1954)
Soldier of Fortune (20th, 1955)
The Tall Men (20th, 1955)
The King and Four Queens (UA, 1956)
Band of Angels (WB, 1957)
Run Silent, Run Deep (UA, 1958)
Teacher's Pet (UA, 1958)

Opposite top: Jack Oakie *(left)* and Clark Gable save Loretta Young in *Call of the Wild*, a tale set in the wilderness during the Alaskan gold rush (United Artists, 1935). **Opposite bottom:** In *Idiot's Delight* Clark Gable is cast as Harry Van, a song and dance man, and Norma Shearer pretends to be a Russian countess trapped in war-torn Europe (MGM, 1939).

But Not for Me (Par., 1959)   *The Misfits* (UA, 1961)
It Started in Naples (Par., 1960)

John Garfield
(1912–1952)

John Garfield *(right)* **returns to Cuba in 1933 to help Jennifer Jones and Gilbert Roland in a revolt against the government in** *We Were Strangers* **(Columbia, 1949).**

As a youth at the Angelo Patri School, John Garfield became interested in boxing and dramatics. Later he studied with Maria Ouspenskaya and Richard Bolesvavsky then joined Eva Le Gallienne's Civic Repertory Theatre. He became an acting member of the Group Theatre appearing in *Waiting for Lefty* and *Awaken and Sing*. In 1932 he married Roberta Seidman and from this union a son, David, and a daughter, Julie, were born. He next appeared on the road with Otto Kruger and then on Broadway with Paul Muni in *Counsellor at Law*. While in the

Gentleman's Agreement, based on Laura Z. Hobson's controversial novel, was Hollywood's first attack on anti–Semitism. It starred Gregory Peck *(left),* Celeste Holm and John Garfield *(center)* (20th Century–Fox, 1947).

hit play *Having a Wonderful Time* he left in the middle of its run to return to the Group Theatre at less salary. While in Cliford Odet's *Golden Boy,* he was signed by Warner Brothers and was cast in the film *Four Daughters,* a surprise hit of 1938 opposite Priscilla Lane. Between his many successful films, he returned to the theatre in *Peer Gynt, Skipper Next to God, Heavenly Express,* and a revival of *Golden Boy.*

John Garfield Film Credits (1933–1951)

Footlight Parade (WB, 1933)
Four Daughters (WB, 1938)
They Made Me a Criminal (WB, 1939)
Blackwell's Island (WB, 1939)
Juarez (WB, 1939)

Daughters Courageous (WB, 1939)
Dust Be My Destiny (WB, 1939)
Castle on the Hudson (WB, 1940)

Saturday's Children (WB, 1940)
Flowing Gold (WB, 1940)
East of the River (WB, 1940)
The Sea Wolf (WB, 1941)
Out of the Fog (WB, 1941)
Dangerously They Live (WB, 1942)
Tortilla Flat(MGM, 1942)
Air Force (WB, 1943)
The Fallen Sparrow (RKO, 1943)
Thank Your Lucky Stars (WB, 1943)
Destination Tokyo (WB, 1943)
Between Two Worlds (WB, 1944)
Hollywood Canteen (WB, 1944)

Pride of the Marines (WB, 1945)
The Postman Always Rings Twice (MGM, 1946)
Nobody Lives Forever (WB, 1946)
Humoresque (WB, 1946)
Body and Soul (UA, 1947)
Gentleman's Agreement (20th, 1947)
Force of Evil (MGM, 1948)
We Were Strangers (Col., 1949)
Jigsaw (unbilled guest appearance; UA, 1949)
Under My Skin (20th, 1950)
The Breaking Point (WB, 1950)
He Ran All the Way (UA, 1951)

Judy Garland
(1922–1969)

She became a vaudeville performer at the age of three in Grand Rapids, Michigan. She and her two sisters formed a group and continued singing in vaudeville until she was thirteen. MGM signed her to a studio contract but she appeared only in a short with Deanna Durbin. Fox borrowed her and there she made one impressive film, *Pigskin Parade.*

Returning to her home studio, she sang "Dear Mr. Gable" in the hit musical *Broadway Melody of 1938* and then became a box office favorite co-starring with Mickey Rooney in the Andy Hardy series. International stardom came to her playing Dorothy and singing "Over the Rainbow in *The Wizard of Oz* at seventeen. For this role she received a special "Oscar" award for her outstanding performance as a juvenile.

Success continued at MGM until she was twenty-eight, when the dual pressures of stardom and personal unhappiness affected her career. After parting with MGM she made a triumphant comeback ap-

Love Finds Andy Hardy has Mickey Rooney again playing Andy and Judy Garland as Betsy Booth, the girl next door (MGM, 1938).

pearing at the London Palladium and the Palace Theatre in New York. Returning to Hollywood, she made the memorable musical *A Star Is Born*. She did television, occasional films and nighclub work until her death in London in 1969.

Judy Garland Feature Films (1936–1963)

Pigskin Parade (20th, 1936)
Broadway Melody of 1938 (MGM, 1937)
Thoroughbreds Don't Cry (MGM, 1937)
Everybody Sing (MGM, 1938)
Listen Darling (MGM, 1938)
Love Finds Andy Hardy (MGM, 1938)
The Wizard of Oz (MGM, 1939)
Babes in Arms (MGM, 1939)

Strike Up the Band (MGM, 1940)
Little Nellie Kelly (MGM, 1940)
Andy Hardy Meets Debutante (MGM, 1940)
Ziegfeld Girl (MGM, 1941)
Life Begins for Andy Hardy (MGM, 1941)
Babes on Broadway (MGM, 1941)

Top: The Wizard of Oz with Judy Garland as Dorothy and Ray Bolger as The Scarecrow is one of the most beloved film fantasy musicals (MGM, 1939). *Bottom:* In *The Pirate* (music by Cole Porter) Judy Garland is a young maiden and Gene Kelly a strolling minstrel who impersonates a pirate. The setting is a Caribbean island in 1820 (MGM, 1948).

For Me and My Gal (MGM, 1942)

Presenting Lily Mars (MGM, 1943)

Girl Crazy (MGM, 1943)

Thousands Cheer (MGM, 1943)

Meet Me in St. Louis (MGM, 1944)

The Clock (MGM, 1945)

The Harvey Girls (MGM, 1946)

Ziegfeld Follies (MGM, 1946)

Till the Clouds Roll By (MGM, 1946)

The Pirate (MGM, 1948)

Easter Parade (MGM, 1948)

Words and Music (MGM, 1948)

In the Good Old Summertime (MGM, 1949)

Summer Stock (MGM, 1950)

A Star Is Born (WB, 1954)

Pepe (voice only; Col., 1960)

Judgement at Nuremberg (UA, 1961)

Gay Purr-ee (voice only; WB, 1962)

A Child Is Waiting (UA, 1963)

I Could Go On Singing (UA, 1963)

Janet Gaynor
(1906–1984)

Janet Gaynor was the first actress to win the Academy Award for best actress (1928) and was nominated again in 1937 but lost to Luise Rainer. During the 1970s she made four appearances presenting the Oscar. The Academy honored her again in 1978 with a special plaque for her contribution to the art of motion pictures as an actress.

Born in Philadelphia, she moved to California and worked at various studios before Irving Cummings cast her in *The Johnston Flood*. Under the Fox banner she became a star and appeared opposite Charles Farrell in twelve films. She married attorney Lydell Peck but they divorced. When her contact ended in 1936 she left the studio to free lance and made only three more successful films.

She married MGM costume designer Gilbert Adrian in 1939 and retired from the movies. They had one son, Robin. After the death of her husband in 1959 she made her stage debut in Joseph Hayes' *The Midnight Sun*. As a painter she was very successful and exhibited in Los Angeles, Chicago and Palm Beach. In 1964 she married producer Paul Gregory.

Gaynor returned to the stage in *Harold and Maude* in 1980. She

Janet Gaynor as Vicki Lester arriving at a premiere with May Robson *(at left with fur),* **Andy Devine and Adolphe Menjou** *(right in top hat)* **in** *A Star Is Born* **(United Artists, 1937).**

appeared on television in a *Love Boat* episode opposite Lew Ayres. She died of pneumonia at 77. Her personal physician thought she had never fully recovered from a terrible automobile accident two years before.

Janet Gaynor Sound Films (1929–1957)

Sunny Side Up (Fox, 1929)
Happy Days (Fox, 1930)
High Society Blues (Fox, 1930)
The Man Who Came Back (Fox, 1930)
Daddy Long Legs (Fox, 1931)
Merely Mary Ann (Fox, 1931)
Delicious (Fox, 1931)
The First Year (Fox, 1932)
Tess of the Storm Country
(Fox, 1932)
State Fair (Fox, 1933)
Adorable (Fox, 1933)
Paddy the Next Best Thing (Fox, 1933)
Carolina (Fox, 1934)
Change of Heart (Fox, 1934)
Servants' Entrance (Fox, 1934)
One More Spring (Fox, 1935)
The Farmer Takes a Wife

Two charming connivers, Janet Gaynor *(left)* and Billie Burke, learn a thing or two about being honest and change their ways in *The Young in Heart* (United Artists, 1938).

(Fox, 1935)
Small Town Girl (Fox, 1936)
Ladies in Love (20th, 1936)
A Star Is Born (UA, 1937)

Three Loves Has Nancy (MGM, 1938)
The Young in Heart (UA, 1938)
Bernadine (20th, 1957)

Betty Grable
(1916–1973)

At the age of fourteen Betty Grable was already dancing in chorus lines of Hollywood musicals. As a young starlet she was under contract to Samuel Goldwyn, RKO and Paramount but without much success. She sang with Ted Fiorito's orchestra and did a vaudeville tour. Unhappy with her career in Hollywood, she accepted a part in the Cole

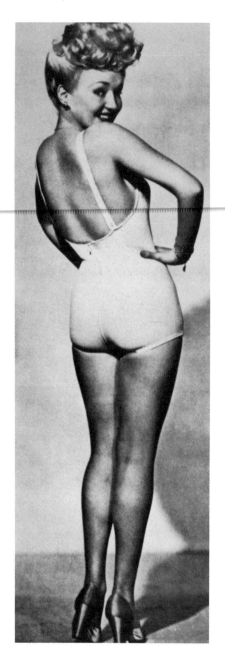

**Betty Grable's famous
World War II pin-up.**

Porter musical *Du Barry Was a Lady* starring Bert Lahr and Ethel Merman. She got excellent reviews and 20th–Century Fox put her under contract. When Alice Faye became ill, she was cast in the star role in *Down Argentina Way*, a technicolor musical which was a big hit. During World War II she reached her pinnacle as the number one pin-up girl with the shapely legs. Her movies were big box office hits. She married bandleader Harry James in 1943 and they had two daughters. Her film career ended in 1955 with the decline of film musicals.

After her divorce from James in 1965 she appeared in Las Vegas and London and toured in stock. She returned to the theatre with great success in the touring version of *Hello, Dolly*. She was to have gone to Australia in *No, No Nanette* but became ill with cancer and died at 57.

Betty Grable Film Credits (1930–1955)

Let's Go Places (Fox, 1930)
New Movietone Follies of 1930 (Fox, 1930)
Whoopee (UA, 1930)
Kiki (UA, 1931)
Palmy Days (UA, 1931)
The Greeks Had a Word for Them (UA, 1932)

Hungarian sisters Jenny and Rosie, played by Betty Grable and June Haver, who become overnight Broadway stars, talk with composer John Payne and Herbert Ashley about their new songs in *The Dolly Sisters* (20th Century–Fox, 1945).

The Kid from Spain (UA, 1932)

Child of Manhattan (Col., 1933)

Probation (Chesterfield, 1932)

Hold 'Em Jail (RKO, 1932)

Cavalcade (Fox, 1933)

What Price Innocence (Col., 1933)

Student Tour (MGM, 1934)

The Gay Divorcee (RKO, 1934)

The Nitwits (RKO, 1935)

Old Man Rhythm (RKO, 1935)

Collegiate (Par., 1935)

Follow the Fleet (RKO, 1936)

Pigskin Parade (20th, 1936)

Don't Turn 'Em Loose (RKO, 1936)

This Way Please (Par., 1937)

Thrill of a Lifetime (Par., 1937)

College Swing (Par., 1938)

Give Me a Sailor (Par., 1938)

Campus Confessions (Par., 1938)

Man About Town (Par., 1939)

Million Dollar Legs (Par., 1939)

The Day the Bookies Wept (RKO, 1939)

Down Argentina Way (20th, 1940)

Tin Pan Alley (20th, 1940)

Moon Over Miami (20th, 1941)

A Yank in the R.A.F. (20th, 1941)

I Wake Up Screaming (20th, 1941)

Footlight Serenade (20th, 1942)

Song of the Islands (20th, 1942)

Springtime in the Rockies (20th, 1942)

Coney Island (20th, 1943)

Four Jills in a Jeep (20th, 1944)

Pin-Up Girl (20th, 1944)

Billy Rose's Diamond Horseshoe (20th, 1945)

The Dolly Sisters (20th, 1945)

Do You Love Me? (unbilled

guest appearance; 20th, 1946)
The Shocking Miss Pilgrim (20th, 1947)
Mother Wore Tights (20th, 1947)
That Lady in Ermine (20th, 1948)
When My Baby Smiles at Me (20th, 1948)
The Beautiful Blonde from Bashful Bend (20th, 1949)
Wabash Avenue (20th, 1950)

My Blue Heaven (20th, 1950)
Call Me Mister (20th, 1951)
Meet Me After the Show (20th, 1951)
The Farmer Takes a Wife (20th, 1953)
How to Marry a Millionaire (20th, 1953)
Three for the Show (Col., 1955)
How to Be Very, Very Popular (20th, 1955)

Cary Grant
(1904–1986)

Cary Grant

At age fifteen Cary Grant joined the Bob Pender Troupe of comics and acrobats in his home town of Bristol, England. With the troupe he toured England and the continent and went to the United States on the Keith vaudeville circuit. When the troupe returned to England Grant remained in the United States and did stints on Coney Island as a barker, stilt-walker and mind reader.

He returned briefly to London where he did several stage roles. In 1927 he went back to New York and appeared in several musicals. The last of these was *Boom, Boom* opposite Jeanette MacDonald. In 1932 he went to Hollywood and B.P. Schulberg signed him to a contract with Paramount where he made routine films until Mae West requested him for her leading man. On loan to RKO he shined with Katharine Hepburn in *Sylvia Scarlett* under the direction of George Cukor. He left Paramount and signed with RKO and Columbia where he achieved stardom with outstanding vehicles, co-stars and directors. In 1942 he became a United States citizen. He was nominated twice for an Oscar. He lost both times but in 1970 he was nominated for a special Oscar. In 1966 he retired from films.

He became an international representative for Faberge and for several years sat on the board of MGM. He first married Virginia Cherril, then heiress Barbara Hutton (1942–45) and actress Betsy Drake (1959–62). From his marriage to Dyan Cannon in 1965 he had a daughter but that marriage also ended in divorce in 1968. He married Barbara Harris in 1981. At the age of 82 he died suddenly of a stroke.

Cary Grant Sound Film Credits (1932–1966)

This Is the Night (Par., 1932)
Sinners in the Sun (Par., 1932)
Merrily We Go to Hell (Par., 1932)
Devil and the Deep (Par., 1932)
Blonde Venus (Par., 1932)
Hot Saturday (Par., 1932)
Madame Butterfly (Par., 1932)
She Done Him Wrong (Par., 1933)
Woman Accused (Par., 1933)
The Eagle and the Hawk (Par., 1933)
Gambling Ship (Par., 1933)

I'm No Angel (Par., 1933)
Alice in Wonderland (Par., 1933)
Thirty-Day Princess (Par., 1934)
Born to Be Bad (UA, 1934)
Kiss and Make Up (Par., 1934)
Ladies Should Listen (Par., 1934)
Enter Madame (Par., 1934)
Wings in the Dark (Par., 1935)
Last Outpost (Par., 1935)
Sylvia Scarlett (RKO, 1935)
Big Brown Eyes (Par., 1936)
Suzy (MGM, 1936)
Wedding Present (Par., 1936)
Amazing Quest (GN, 1936)

The Awful Truth with Cary Grant and Irene Dunne was a superb production which became the epitome of the screwball comedies of the 1930's (Columbia, 1937).

When You're in Love (Col., 1937)

Toast of New York (RKO, 1937)

Topper (MGM, 1937)

The Awful Truth (Col., 1937)

Bringing Up Baby (RKO, 1938)

Holiday (Col., 1938)

Gunga Din (RKO, 1939)

Only Angels Have Wings (Col., 1939)

In Name Only (RKO, 1939)

His Girl Friday (Col., 1940)

My Favorite Wife (RKO, 1940)

Unjustly accused Cary Grant escapes from jail and takes refuge in Jean Arthur's home in *Talk of the Town* (Columbia, 1942).

The Howards of Virginia (Col., 1940)

The Philadelphia Story (MGM, 1940)

Penny Serenade (Col., 1941)

Suspicion (RKO, 1941)

Talk of the Town (Col., 1942)

Once Upon a Honeymoon (RKO, 1942)

Mr. Lucky (RKO, 1943)

Destination Tokyo (WB, 1943)

Once Upon a Time (Col., 1944)

Arsenic and Old Lace (WB, 1944)

None But the Lonely Heart (RKO, 1944)

Night and Day (WB, 1946)
Without Reservations (unbilled guest appearance; RKO, 1946)
Notorious (RKO, 1946)
The Bachelor and the Bobby-Soxer (RKO, 1947)
The Bishop's Wife (RKO, 1947)
Mr. Blandings Builds His Dream House (RKO, 1948)
Every Girl Should Be Married (RKO, 1948)
I Was a Male War Bride (20th, 1949)
Crisis (MGM, 1950)
People Will Talk (20th, 1951)
Room for One More (WB, 1952)
Monkey Business (20th, 1952)

Dream Wife (MGM, 1953)
To Catch a Thief (Par., 1955)
The Pride and the Passion (UA, 1957)
An Affair to Remember (20th, 1957)
Kiss Them for Me (20th, 1957)
Indiscreet (WB, 1958)
Houseboat (Par., 1958)
North by Northwest (MGM, 1959)
Operation Petticoat (Univ., 1959)
The Grass Is Greener (Univ., 1960)
That Touch of Mink (Univ., 1962)
Charade (Univ., 1963)
Father Goose (Univ., 1964)
Walk, Don't Run (Col., 1966)

Ann Harding
(1902–1981)

Daughter of a United States Army officer, she was born at Fort Sam Houston, Texas, and grew up in Illinois, Cuba and New Jersey, where her father was stationed. She first appeared with Greenwich Village's Provincetown Players, then in stock in Detroit and Philadelphia. She then went on to Broadway where she became a star in such plays as *Tarnish, Thoroughbred,* and *Trial of Mary Dugan,* which ran over two seasons.

Pathé signed her for her film debut in *Paris Bound,* with many successes to follow. In 1937 she starred in George Bernard Shaw's play *Candida,* which was a great hit in London. She returned to Hollywood to appear in more films and also returned to Broadway to appear in *Goodbye My Fancy* and Tennesse Williams' *Garden District.* On television she was in such shows as *Armstrong Circle Theatre, Burke's Law, Ben Casey,* and *The Defenders.*

Top: Ann Harding leaves her husband *(pictured)* and takes up with a musician but returns to her husband (Frank Fenton) in *Paris Bound* (Pathé, 1929). *Bottom:* Louis Calhern stars as Supreme Court Justice Oliver Wendell Holmes in *The Magnificent Yankee* with Ann Harding as his wife (MGM, 1950).

Ann Harding Film Credits (1929–1956)

Paris Bound (Pathé, 1929)
Her Private Affair (Pathé, 1929)
Condemned (UA, 1929)
Holiday (Pathé, 1930)
Girl of the Golden West (WB, 1930)
East Lynne (Fox, 1931)
Devotion (RKO, 1931)
Prestige (RKO, 1932)
Westward Passage (RKO, 1932)
The Conquerors (RKO, 1932)
The Animal Kingdom (RKO, 1932)
When Ladies Meet (MGM, 1933)
Double Harness (RKO, 1933)
Right to Romance (RKO, 1933)
Gallant Lady (UA, 1933)
Life of Vergie Winters (RKO, 1934)
The Fountain (RKO, 1934)
Biography of a Bachelor Girl (MGM, 1935)
Enchanted April (RKO, 1935)
The Flame Within (MGM, 1935)

Peter Ibbetson (Par., 1935)
The Lady Consents (RKO, 1936)
The Witness Chair (RKO, 1936)
Love from a Stranger (UA, 1937)
Eyes in the Night (MGM, 1942)
Mission to Moscow (WB, 1943)
The North Star (RKO, 1943)
Janie (WB, 1944)
Nine Girls (Col., 1944)
Those Endearing Young Charms (RKO, 1945)
Janie Gets Married (WB, 1946)
It Happened on Fifth Avenue (AA, 1947)
Christmas Eve (UA, 1947)
The Magnificent Yankee (MGM, 1950)
Two Weeks with Love (MGM, 1950)
The Unknown Man (MGM, 1951)
The Man in the Gray Flannel Suit (20th, 1956)
I've Lived Before (Univ., 1956)
Strange Intruder (AA, 1956)

Jean Harlow
(1911–1937)

Jean Harlow was born in Kansas City, Missouri, where her father was a dentist. At the age of sixteen she ran away from school and married. After a short time she was divorced and moved with her mother and father-in-law to California where she found extra work in films. She next worked in comedy shorts with Laurel and Hardy and in featured films. Her big break came when Howard Hughes signed her as a cast replacement for Greta Nissen in the epic airplane film *Hell's Angels*. It made her a star. Under Hughes she was lent out to various studios and worked with Frank Capra, Spencer Tracy and Clark Gable. Hughes

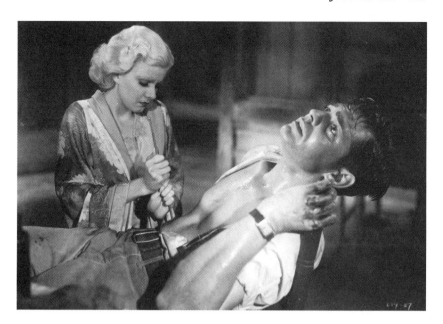

Top: Jean Harlow removing a bullet from Clark Gable's abdomen in *Red Dust*, a drama set in the exotic background of a rubber plantation in the Far East (MGM, 1932). *Bottom:* Jean Harlow is a showgirl in London and Cary Grant is the dashing aviator she meets in *Suzy* (MGM, 1936).

sold her contract to MGM. With that studio's guidance she became a top star within two years.

Her next brief marriage to MGM executive Paul Bern ended when he committed suicide. Her third marriage to Paul Rosson ended in divorce after one year.

During the filming of *Saratoga* she died, at twenty-six, and the film was completed with a double. It was released after her death and was one of the top grossers of 1937.

Jean Harlow Sound Feature Films (1929–1937)

The Love Parade (Par., 1929)
The Saturday Night Kid (Par., 1929)
Hell's Angels (UA, 1930)
The Secret Six (MGM, 1931)
Iron Man (Univ., 1931)
Public Enemy (WB, 1931)
Goldie (Fox, 1931)
Platinum Blonde (Col., 1931)
Three Wise Girls (Col., 1932)
The Beast of the City (MGM, 1932)
Red-Headed Woman (MGM, 1932)
Red Dust (MGM, 1932)
Dinner at Eight (MGM, 1933)
Hold Your Man (MGM, 1933)
Bombshell (MGM, 1933)
The Girl from Missouri (MGM, 1934)
Reckless (MGM, 1935)
China Seas (MGM, 1935)
Riffraff (MGM, 1935)
Wife vs. Secretary (MGM, 1936)
Suzy (MGM, 1936)
Libeled Lady (MGM, 1936)
Personal Property (MGM, 1937)
Saratoga (MGM, 1937)

Susan Hayward
(1918–1975)

Susan Hayward was born in Brooklyn, New York, the daughter of a city transit worker. She attended a commercial high school where she took courses in dress design. She worked as a fashion model before going to Hollywood where she was first a contract player and later became a star.

She was nominated five times for the Academy Award and finally won it for her performance in *I Want to Live* in 1958.

She married actor Jess Barker and they had twin sons. This union

Susan Hayward plays Barbara Graham whose sensational trial brought her a conviction and the death sentence in *I Want to Live*, with Simon Oakland as a reporter (United Artists, 1958).

NO WAY!

lasted ten years before they were divorced in 1954. She later married businessman F. Eaton Chalkley in 1957 and lived in Carrollton, Georgia, until his death in 1966. They had a winter home in Ft. Lauderdale, Florida.

She died in California of a brain tumor at the age of 56.

Susan Hayward Feature Films (1937–1972)

Hollywood Hotel (WB, 1937)
The Sisters (WB, 1938)
Comet Over Broadway (WB, 1938)
Girls on Probation (WB, 1938)
Beau Geste (Par., 1939)
Our Leading Citizen (Par., 1939)
$1,000 a Touchdown (Par., 1939)
Adam Had Four Sons (Col., 1941)
Sis Hopkins (Rep., 1941)

Among the Living (Par., 1941)
Reap the Wild Wind (Par., 1942)
Forest Rangers (Par., 1942)
I Married a Witch (UA, 1942)
Star Spangled Banner (Par., 1942)
Hit Parade of 1943 (Rep., 1943)
Young and Willing (UA, 1943)
Jack London (UA, 1943)
The Fighting Seabees (Rep., 1944)

Susan Hayward and Michael Connors star in the adaptation of Harold Robbins' sensational novel *Where Love Has Gone* (Paramount, 1964).

The Hairy Ape (UA, 1944)
And Now Tomorrow (Par., 1944)
Deadline at Dawn (RKO, 1946)
Canyon Passage (Univ., 1946)
Smash-Up, the Story of a Woman (Univ., 1947)
The Lost Moment (Univ., 1947)
They Won't Believe Me (RKO, 1947)
Tap Roots (Univ., 1948)
The Saxon Charm (Univ., 1948)
Tulsa (EL, 1949)
House of Strangers (20th, 1949)
My Foolish Heart (RKO, 1949)
I'd Climb the Highest Mountain (20th, 1951)
Rawhide (20th, 1951)
I Can Get It for You Wholesale (20th, 1951)
David and Bathsheba (20th, 1951)
With a Song in My Heart (20th, 1952)
The Snows of Kilimanjaro (20th, 1952)
The Lusty Men (RKO, 1952)
The President's Lady (20th, 1953)
White Witch Doctor (20th, 1953)
Demetrius and the Gladiators (20th, 1954)
Garden of Evil (20th, 1954)
Untamed (20th, 1955)
Soldier of Fortune (20th, 1955)
I'll Cry Tomorrow (MGM, 1955)
The Conqueror (RKO, 1956)
Top Secret Affair (WB, 1957)

I Want to Live (UA, 1958)
Woman Obsessed (20th, 1959)
Thunder in the Sun (Par., 1959)
The Marriage-Go-Round (20th, 1960)
Ada (MGM, 1961)
Back Street (Univ., 1961)

I Thank a Fool (MGM, 1962)
Stolen Hours (UA, 1963)
Where Love Has Gone (Par., 1964)
The Honey Pot (UA, 1967)
Valley of the Dolls (20th, 1967)
The Revengers (NGP, 1972)

Rita Hayworth (1918–1987)

Her father, Eduardo Casino, was a Spanish-born dancer and her mother, Volga Haworth, was a Ziegfeld Follies showgirl. At the age of 12 she began dancing professionally in her father's act under the name of Rita Casino. While performing in Mexico she was signed by Fox Film Company and appeared in films for that studio. At 18 she married Edward Judson. As her manager he won her a seven-year contract at Columbia Pictures. Her name was changed to Rita Hayworth there and she was groomed for stardom. Her second husband was Orson Wells. They had a daughter, Rebecca. In 1949 she married Prince Aly Khan and from that union a daughter, Yasmin, was born. On the screen she appeared opposite Cary Grant, Fred Astaire, Gene Kelly, Glenn Ford, Burt Lancaster, James Cagney, Gary Cooper, Frank Sinatra and Tyrone Power. After her divorce from Khan she married singer Dick Haymes. This marriage also failed. Her last marriage to movie producer James Hill ended in divorce after four years.

In 1981 she was legally declared unable to care for herself and was placed in the care of her daughter, Princess Yasmin, who took her to New York and cared for her until her death from Alzheimer's disease at the age of 68.

Rita Hayworth Feature Films (1935–1972)

As Rita Casino:
    Dante's Inferno (Fox, 1935)
    Under the Pampas Moon (Fox, 1935)

Charlie Chan in Egypt (Fox, 1935)
Paddy O'Day (Fox, 1935)
Human Cargo (Fox, 1936)

Rita Hayworth as *Miss Sadie Thompson* shows up on a Pacific island just after World War II to be greeted by the U.S. Marines (Columbia, 1953).

A Message to Garcia (Fox, 1936)
Meet Neto Wolfe (Col., 1936)
Rebellion (Crescent, 1936)
Old Louisiana (Crescent, 1937)
Hit the Saddle (Rep., 1937)
Trouble in Texas (GN, 1937)

As Rita Hayworth:
Criminals of the Air (Col., 1937)
Girls Can Play (Col., 1937)
The Game That Kills (Col., 1937)
Paid to Dance (Col., 1937)
The Shadow (Col., 1937)
Who Killed Gail Preston? (Col., 1938)
There's Always a Woman (Col., 1938)
Convicted (Col., 1938)

Juvenile Court (Col., 1938)
Homicide Bureau (Col., 1939)
The Lone Wolf Spy Hunt (Col., 1939)
Renegade Ranger (RKO, 1939)
Only Angels Have Wings (Col., 1939)
Special Inspector (Syndicate, 1939)
Music in My Heart (Col., 1940)
Blondie on a Budget (Col., 1940)
Susan and God (MGM, 1940)
The Lady in Question (Col., 1940)
Angels Over Broadway (Col., 1940)
Strawberry Blonde (WB, 1941)
Affectionately Yours (WB, 1941)

Rita Hayworth's famous World War II pin-up.

Blood and Sand (20th, 1941)
You'll Never Get Rich (Col., 1941)
My Gal Sal (20th, 1942)
Tales of Manhattan (20th, 1942)
You Were Never Lovelier (Col., 1942)
Cover Girl (Col., 1944)
Tonight and Every Night (Col., 1945)
Gilda (Col., 1946)

Down to Earth (Col., 1947)
The Lady from Shanghai (Col., 1948)
The Loves of Carmen (Col., 1948)
Affair in Trinidad (Col., 1952)
Salome (Col., 1953)
Miss Sadie Thompson (Col., 1953)
Fire Down Below (Col., 1957)
Pal Joey (Col., 1957)

Separate Tables (UA,, 1958)
They Came to Cordura (Col., 1959)
The Story on Page One (Col., 1959)
The Happy Thieves (UA, 1962)
Circus World (Par., 1965)

The Money Trap (MGM, 1966)
The Rover (ABC, 1968)
Sons of Satan (Foreign, 1969)
The Road to Saline (Foreign, 1970)
The Naked Zoo (Foreign, 1971)
The Wrath of God (MGM, 1972)

Sonja Henie
(1912–1969)

In *Second Fiddle* Sonja Henie *(hat)* plays a Minnesota school teacher who is brought to Hollywood by Tyrone Power *(left)* to star in a film. Edna May Oliver and Rudy Vallee look on (20th Century–Fox, 1939).

Sonja Henie was born in Oslo, Norway, and began dancing at the age of four, ice skating at eight, and at 15 she was a world champion on skates. In the Olympic Games of 1928, 1932 and 1936 she won gold medals and broke world records. She turned professional in her own ice

Sonja Henie

shows and while on tour in Los Angeles Darryl Zanuck signed her to a contract. Her first film was a success and she worked for 20th Century and toured in her ice shows until 1943. After leaving the studio she continued to star and tour in her own ice revues. She returned to the movies for three final films — one each at RKO and Universal and one in London. In 1960 she retired from show business a wealthy woman and died nine years later from leukemia.

Sonja Henie Feature Films (1936–1958)

One in a Million (20th, 1936)
Thin Ice (20th, 1937)
Happy Landing (20th, 1938)
My Lucky Star (20th, 1938)
Second Fiddle (20th, 1939)
Everything Happens at Night
  (20th, 1939)

Sun Valley Serenade (20th, 1941)
Iceland (20th, 1942)
Wintertime (20th, 1943)
It's a Pleasure (RKO, 1945)
The Countess of Monte Cristo
  (Univ., 1948)
Hello, London (BIP, 1958)

Miriam Hopkins
(1902–1972)

The Heiress, a compelling drama based on a Henry James novel, starred Montgomery Clift as the suitor and Miriam Hopkins as the aunt (Paramount, 1949).

Miriam Hopkins was born in Savannah, Georgia, in 1902 and made her debut as a chorus girl in Irving Berlin's *Music Box Revue* in 1921. In 1923 she earned rave reviews for her appearance in the play *Little Jesse James*. From then until 1931 she gained stardom in many successful Broadway plays and appeared on the London stage in one vehicle.

Bette Davis and Mirian Hopkins play cousins with a deep secret in *The Old Maid* (Warner Bros., 1939).

She signed a contract with Paramount and made routine pictures until she played Ivy the barmaid in *Dr. Jekyll and Mr. Hyde* which led to better roles on the Paramount lot and loan-outs to other studios. When her contract ended she returned to Broadway, replacing an ill Tallulah Bankhead in *Jezebel*. She went back to Hollywood under contract to Samuel Goldwyn and made four successful films with two loan-outs to RKO. She returned again to the stage to tour in *Wine of Choice*. She then signed with Warner Brothers where she made numerous successful films. Back on Broadway, she replaced Tallulah Bankhead again in *Skin of Our Teeth*.

Over the years she remained a stage actress but returned to Hollywood occasionally in supporting roles in top productions with renowned directors. She died of a massive heart attack in 1972.

Miriam Hopkins Sound Film Credits (1930–1969)

Fast and Loose (Par., 1930)

The Smiling Lieutenant (Par., 1931)

24 Hours (Par., 1931)

Dr. Jekyll and Mr. Hyde (Par., 1932)

Two Kinds of Women (Par., 1932)

Dancers in the Dark (Par., 1932)

The World and the Flesh (Par., 1932)

Trouble in Paradise (Par., 1932)

The Story of Temple Drake (Par., 1933)

Design for Living (Par., 1933)

Stranger's Return (MGM, 1933)

All of Me (Par., 1934)

She Loves Me Not (Par., 1934)

The Richest Girl in the World (RKO, 1934)

Becky Sharp (RKO, 1935)

Barbary Coast (UA, 1935)

Splendor (UA, 1935)

These Three (UA, 1936)

Men Are Not Gods (UA, 1937)

The Woman I Love (RKO, 1937)

Woman Chases Man (UA, 1937)

Wise Girl (RKO, 1937)

The Old Maid (WB, 1939)

Virginia City (WB, 1940)

The Lady with Red Hair (WB, 1940)

A Gentleman After Dark (UA, 1942)

Old Acquaintance (WB, 1943)

The Heiress (Par., 1949)

The Mating Season (Par., 1951)

Carrie (Par., 1952)

Outcasts of Poker Flat (20th, 1952)

The Children's Hour (UA, 1962)

Fannie Hill: Memoirs of a Woman of Pleasure (Favorite Films, 1965)

The Chase (Col., 1966)

Comeback (never released, 1969)

Leslie Howard
(1893–1943)

Leslie Howard's parents were Hungarian immigrants who became British citizens. He studied at Dulwich College and worked in a bank until he went into service in World War I. In 1917 he was shell-shocked

Humphrey Bogart *(left)* as gangster Duke Mantee, Leslie Howard as an idealistic writer and Bette Davis as Gabrielle are caught in *The Petrified Forest* (Warner Bros., 1936).

at the front and sent home. As a form of therapy he became involved in local theatre. From that experience he joined a theatre company and went on tour. For a brief time he did some work in silent films and went on to make a name for himself on the London stage. Coming to Broadway, he acted in several hit plays and appeared opposite Katherine Cornell. He returned to England to play opposite Edna Best and Tallulah Bankhead.

Warner Brothers signed him to a contract. During the '30s he appeared with many glamorous leading ladies such as Norma Shearer, Marion Davies, Ann Harding, Mary Pickford, Bette Davis, Ingrid Bergman and Vivien Leigh. He returned to the theatre as an actor, director and producer.

During World War II he went back to England and worked in films there. He went on a lecture tour for the British government and died when his plane, which German Intelligence thought held Winston Churchill, was shot down by the Nazis after leaving Lisbon.

Having saved Ashley (Leslie Howard, *right*) from being arrested, Rhett Butler (Clark Gable) is met at the door by Melanie (Olivia de Havilland) as Ward Bond *(left)* tells of the raid on shantytown in *Gone With the Wind* (MGM, 1939).

Leslie Howard Feature Films (1930–1942)

Outward Bound (WB, 1930)
Never the Twain Shall Meet (MGM, 1931)
A Free Soul (MGM, 1931)
Five and Ten (MGM, 1931)
Devotion (RKO, 1931)
Reserved for Ladies (Par., 1932)
Smilin' Through (MGM, 1932)
The Animal Kingdom (RKO, 1932)
Secrets (UA, 1933)
Captured (WB, 1933)
Berkeley Square (Fox, 1933)
The Lady Is Willing (Col., 1934)
Of Human Bondage (RKO, 1934)

British Agent (WB, 1934)
The Scarlet Pimpernel (UA, 1935)
The Petrified Forest (WB, 1936)
Romeo and Juliet (MGM, 1936)
It's Love I'm After (WB, 1937)
Stand-In (UA, 1937)
Pygmalion (MGM, 1938)
Gone with the Wind (MGM, 1939)
Intermezzo (UA, 1939)
The First of the Few (Spitfire; King, 1941)
Pimpernel Smith (UA, 1942)
The Invaders (Col., 1942)

Al Jolson
(1886–1950)

Al Jolson was born in Russia and came to the United States as a young child. His father was a cantor and Al first sang in a synagogue. He ran away from home, joined a circus, and entered nightclub work and vaudeville as a singer. He first wore blackface make-up in a minstrel show.

After appearing in two Broadway shows with Gaby Deslys he signed a contract with the Shuberts. For them he appeared in many hit musicals and also became a recording star. When Warners produced *The Jazz Singer* they signed him to a contract. He returned to Broadway in *Wonder Bar* and successfully began radio work. During World War II he entertained the troops. Columbia made two successful films of his life in which he dubbed the songs for Larry Parks who played Jolson.

He entertained troops again during the Korean conflict. At sixty-four he died of a heart attack and film projects planned for him at RKO were cancelled.

Al Jolson Feature Films (1927–1949)

The Jazz Singer (WB, 1927)
Singing Fool (WB, 1928)
Sonny Boy (WB, 1929)
Say It with Songs (WB, 1929)
Mammy (WB, 1930)
Big Boy (WB, 1930)
Hallelujah, I'm a Bum (UA, 1933)
Wonder Bar (WB, 1934)
Go into Your Dance (WB, 1935)

The Singing Kid (WB, 1936)
Rose of Washington Square (20th, 1939)
Hollywood Cavalcade (20th, 1939)
Swanee River (20th, 1939)
Rhaposody in Blue (WB, 1945)
The Jolson Story (voice only; Col., 1946)
Jolson Sings Again (voice only; Col., 1949)

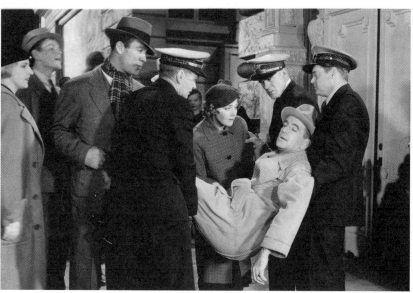

Top: In *The Jazz Singer*, which ushered in sound films in 1927, May McAvoy and Al Jolson become movie sensations (Warner Bros., 1927). *Bottom:* Ruby Keeler and Al Jolson *(being carried)* star in the backstage musical *Go into Your Dance* with outstanding music and lyrics by Harry Warren and Al Dubin (Warner Bros., 1935).

Grace Kelly
(1928–1982)

Grace Kelly

Grace Kelly was born the daughter of a multi-millionaire in Philadelphia. After attending Ravenhill Academy and graduating from Stevens School in 1947, she studied at the American Academy of Dramatic Art in New York for two years. During this time she worked as a top fashion model and appeared on the covers of leading magazines. She worked briefly in stock and appeared in television plays before

William Holden is a naval officer recalled to active duty and Grace Kelly is his wife in *The Bridges at Toko-Ri*, based on a James Michener novel (Paramount, 1954).

making her Broadway debut in 1949 opposite Raymond Massey. Her second film, *High Noon,* resulted in a seven-year contract with MGM. On loan-outs to other studios she became an important star and won the Oscar for her performance in *The Country Girl* in 1954. In 1956 she married Prince Rainier III of Monaco. They had three children—Caroline, Albert and Stephanie. Over the years she devoted considerable time to Monegasque and international charities and cultural activities. From 1976 to 1981 she served on the board of directors of 20th–Century Fox. She died in Monaco at the age of 52 of a cerebral hemorrhage after being injured in an automobile accident.

Grace Kelly Feature Films (1951–1956)

Fourteen Hours (20th, 1951)
High Noon (UA, 1952)
Mogambo (MGM, 1953)
Dial M for Murder (WB, 1954)
Rear Window (Par., 1954)
The Country Girl (Par., 1954)

Green Fire (MGM, 1954)
The Bridges at Toko-Ri (Par., 1954)
To Catch a Thief (Par., 1955)
The Swan (MGM, 1956)
High Society (MGM, 1956)

Alan Ladd
(1913–1964)

Alan Ladd was born in Hot Springs, Arkansas, and reared in California. In high school he excelled in sports even though he was small compared to other athletes. After high school he worked at odd jobs and was a handyman at Warner Brothers for two years before doing bit roles in films, radio and local theatre productions. Actress Sue Carol became his agent and guided his career. They were married in 1942 after his divorce from his first wife. They had two children, David and Alana. His eldest son, Alan Ladd, Jr., is from his first marriage. Under Sue Carol's management he became one of Paramount's most popular stars for many years. After his contract with Paramount expired, he signed with Warner Brothers, Universal and Columbia, and also made films for his own company, Jaguar. He died of a gunshot wound which was determined to be accidental in 1964.

Alan Ladd Feature Films (1932–1964)

Once in a Lifetime (Univ., 1932)
Pigskin Parade (20th, 1936)
Last Train from Madrid (Par., 1936)
Souls at Sea (Par., 1937)
Hold 'Em Navy (Par. 1937)
The Goldwyn Follies (UA, 1938)
Come On Leathernecks (Rep., 1938)

The Green Hornet (Univ. serial, 1939)
Rulers of the Sea (Par., 1939)
Beast of Berlin (PRC, 1939)
Gangs of Chicago (Rep., 1940)
Light of Western Stars (Par., 1940)
In Old Missouri (Rep., 1940)

Top: Alan Ladd *(right)* is the doctor who grew up on the wrong side of the tracks and returns home to practice medicine. Loretta Young is a patient of doctor Cecil Kellaway in *And Now Tomorrow* (Paramount, 1944). *Bottom:* Alan Ladd and Veronica Lake, one of the great love teams of the 1940's, in *Saigon*, a thriller which was their last picture together (Paramount, 1948).

Mystery thriller *The Blue Dahlia* cast Alan Ladd as a returning G.I. and Doris Dowling as his unfaithful wife (Paramount, 1946).

The Howards of Virginia (Col., 1940)
Those Were the Days (Par., 1940)
Captain Caution (UA, 1940)
Wildcat Bus (RKO, 1940)
Meet the Missus (Rep., 1940)
Great Guns (20th, 1941)
Citizen Kane (RKO, 1941)
Cadet Girl (20th, 1941)
Petticoat Politics (Rep., 1941)
The Black Cat (Univ., 1941)
The Reluctant Dragon (RKO, 1941)
Paper Bullets (PRC, 1941)
Joan of Paris (RKO, 1942)
This Gun for Hire (Par., 1942)
The Glass Key (Par., 1942)
Lucky Jordan (Par., 1942)

Star Spangled Rhythm (Par., 1942)
China (Par., 1943)
And Now Tomorrow (Par., 1944)
Salty O'Rourke (Par., 1945)
Duffy's Tavern (Par., 1945)
The Blue Dahlia (Par., 1946)
O.S.S. (Par., 1946)
Two Years Before the Mast (Par., 1946)
Calcutta (Par., 1947)
Variety Girl (Par., 1947)
Wild Harvest (Par., '1947)
My Favorite Brunette (unbilled guest appearance; Par., 1947)
Saigon (Par., 1948)
Beyond Glory (Par., 1948)
Whispering Smith (Par., 1948)
The Great Gatsby (Par., 1949)

Chicago Deadline (Par., 1949)
Captain Carey, U.S.A. (Par., 1950)
Branded (Par., 1951)
Appiontment with Danger (Par., 1951)
Red Mountain (Par., 1952)
The Iron Mistress (WB, 1952)
Thunder in the East (Par., 1953)
Desert Legion (Univ., 1953)
Shane (Par., 1953)
Botany Bay (Par., 1953)
Paratrooper (Col., 1954)
Saskatchewan (Univ., 1954)
Hell Below Zero (Col., 1954)
The Black Knight (Col., 1954)
Drum Beat (Col., 1954)

The McConnell Story (WB, 1955)
Hell on Frisco Bay (WB, 1955)
Santiago (WB, 1956)
The Big Land (WB, 1957)
Boy on a Dolphin (20th, 1957)
The Deep Six (WB, 1958)
The Proud Rebel (BV, 1958)
The Badlanders (MGM, 1958)
The Man in the Net (UA, 1959)
Guns of the Timberland (WB, 1960)
All the Young Men (Col., 1960)
One Foot in Hell (20th, 1960)
13 West Street (Col., 1962)
The Carpetbaggers (Par., 1964)

Mario Lanza
(1921–1959)

Mario Lanza was born in South Philadelphia and took singing lessons as a child. Not interested in academic studies, he dropped out of high school to work in his grandfather's wholesale grocery business. In 1942 he had an audition with conductor Serge Koussevitzsky which resulted in a scholarship and an appearance at the Berkshire Summer Festival in Tanglewood, Massachusetts. He was drafted into the Army Air Force, took his basic training in Miami, Florida, and was stationed at Marfa Air Force Base in Texas. At that base he was cast in Frank Loesser's musical *On the Beam.* It went on tour and one critic referred to Lanza as *the Caruso of the Air Force.* In 1945 he was discharged from the service and married Betty Hicks. He signed a recording contract with RCA Victor and under the management of Columbia Concerts of New York he toured the United States. His last engagement on the tour was at the Hollywood Bowl where he came to the attention of Louis B. Mayer and consequently signed a contract with MGM. He became an overnight star and his films broke box office records. He died of a heart attack in a Rome clinic at the age of 38.

Top: Kathryn Grayson is an opera star, Mario Lanza *(center)* a rough-and-ready fisherman and David Niven the manager of an opera company in *The Toast of New Orleans.* (MGM, 1950). *Bottom:* At the stage door *The Great Caruso* (Mario Lanza, *center with hat off*) and his friends meet Ann Blyth (MGM, 1951).

Mario Lanza Feature Films (1949–1959)

The Midnight Kiss (MGM, 1949)
The Toast of New Orleans
  (MGM, 1950)
The Great Caruso (MGM, 1951)
Because You're Mine (MGM,
  1952)

The Student Prince (voice only;
  MGM, 1954)
Serenade (WB, 1956)
The Seven Hills of Rome (MGM,
  1958)
For the First Time (MGM, 1959)

Charles Laughton
(1899–1962)

Charles Laughton was born in Scarborough, England, and educated at Stonyhurst College. During World War I he was in the service. After the war he worked in the family hotel business. He joined an acting company, then enrolled at the Royal Academy of Dramatic Art. In 1926 he made his London debut in a play with Elsa Lanchester whom he married ten years later. They appeared together in film shorts and he was soon seen in featured films in England. He and Elsa came to Broadway under Gilbert Miller's banner in the successful play *Payment Deferred*. Next he appeared as a star in the play *Alibi* for the same producer and Paramount signed him to a term contract. In 1933 he won an Academy Award for the Alexander Korda film *The Private Life of Henry VIII*. He became a film director in the outstanding *The Night of the Hunter*. He returned to the theatre to direct and star in *Don Juan in Hell*, direct *John Brown's Body* and do solo performances of famous readings. His skill as a director also showed in the play *The Caine Mutiny Trial*. He and Elsa appeared at Stratford-Upon-Avon and West End theatres, giving outstanding performances. They were both nominated for Oscars for their work together in *Witness for the Prosecution*. He died in 1962 from cancer after filming *Advise and Consent*.

Charles Laughton Sound Feature Films (1929–1962)

Piccadilly (BIP, 1929)
Wolves (British and Dominion

Productions, 1930)
Down River (GB, 1931)

The British film industry's first great release outside the empire was *The Private Life of Henry VIII*, produced and directed by Alexander Korda. Charles Laughton was the famous monarch. The child is not credited (United Artists, 1933).

The Old Dark House (Univ., 1932)
Devil and the Deep (Par., 1932)
Payment Deferred (MGM, 1932)
The Sign of the Cross (Par., 1932)
If I Had a Million (Par., 1932)
Island of Lost Souls (Par., 1933)
The Private Life of Henry VIII (UA, 1933)
White Woman (Par., 1933)
The Barretts of Wimpole Street (MGM, 1934)
Ruggles of Red Gap (Par., 1935)
Les Miserables (UA, 1935)
Mutiny on the Bounty (MGM, 1935)

Allen Drury's novel *Advise and Consent* was a study of high politics in Washington. The film adaptation starred Charles Laughton *(left)* and Walter Pidgeon (Columbia, 1962).

Rembrandt (London Films, 1936)
Vessel of Wrath (Par., 1938)
St. Martin's Lane (Par., 1939)
Jamaica Inn (Par., 1939)
The Hunchback of Notre Dame (RKO, 1939)
They Knew What They Wanted (RKO, 1940)
It Started with Eve (Univ., 1941)
The Tuttles of Tahiti (RKO, 1942)
Tales of Manhattan (20th, 1942)
Stand By for Action (MGM, 1942)
Forever and a Day (RKO, 1943)
This Land Is Mine (RKO, 1943)
The Man from Down Under (MGM, 1943)
The Canterville Ghost (MGM, 1944)
The Suspect (Univ., 1944)
Captain Kidd (UA, 1945)
Because of Him (Univ., 1946)
The Paradine Case (Selznick, 1948)
The Big Clock (Par., 1948)
Arch of Triumph (UA, 1948)
The Girl from Manhattan (UA, 1948)
The Bribe (MGM, 1949)
The Man on the Eiffel Tower (RKO, 1949)
The Blue Veil (RKO, 1951)
The Strange Door (Univ., 1951)

O. Henry's Full House (20th, 1952)
Abbott and Costello Meet Captain Kidd (WB, 1952)
Salome (Col., 1953)
Young Bess (MGM, 1953)

Hobson's Choice (UA, 1954)
Witness for the Prosecution (UA, 1957)
Under Ten Flags (Par., 1960)
Spartacus (Univ., 1960)
Advise and Consent (Col., 1962)

Vivien Leigh
(1913–1967)

A Streetcar Named Desire **(from Tennessee Williams' hit Broadway play) cast Vivien Leigh as the ill-fated Blanche DuBois and Marlon Brando as macho Stanley (Warner Bros., 1951).**

Vivien Leigh was born in India and educated in England and on the continent. She married a barrister, then attended the Royal Academy of Dramatic Art for a brief time and appeared in a few films before her theatre debut in London. Alexander Korda saw her on stage and signed her to a film contract. She played opposite Lawrence Olivier in two films and continued stage appearances. In following films she appeared opposite Charles Laughton, Conrad Veidt and Robert Taylor.

Clark Gable as dashing Rhett Butler and Vivien Leigh as beautiful and headstrong Scarlet O'Hara aboard a ship sailing for New Orleans on their honeymoon in *Gone with the Wind* (MGM, 1939).

She came to the United States and David Selznick cast her as Scarlett O'Hara in *Gone with the Wind* which won her an Academy Award in 1939. After her divorce she married Lawrence Olivier. They both returned to England during the war years but she made no stage or film appearances because of her contract with Selznick and her poor health. In 1945 her contract with Selznick was declared invalid and she returned to the theatre and films. She won her second Oscar in 1951 for Blanche in *A Streetcar Named Desire* opposite Marlon Brando. In 1960 she divorced Olivier. She continued making occasional films and touring in plays until her death in 1967.

Vivien Leigh Feature Films (1934–1965)

Things Are Looking Up (Gainsborough, 1934)
The Village Squire (British and Dominions, 1935)
Gentleman's Agreement (British and Dominions, 1935)
Look Up and Laugh (Associated Talking Pictures, 1935)
Fire Over England (UA, 1937)
Dark Journey (UA, 1937)
Storm in a Teacup (UA, 1937)
A Yank at Oxford (MGM, 1938)
St. Martin's Lane ("The Sidewalks of London" Par., 1938)
Gone with the Wind (MGM, 1939)
Waterloo Bridge (MGM, 1940)
Twenty-one Days Together (Col., 1940)
That Hamilton Woman (UA, 1941)
Caesar and Cleopatra (UA, 1946)
Anna Karenina (20th, 1948)
A Streetcar Named Desire (WB, 1951)
The Deep Blue Sea (20th, 1955)
The Roman Spring of Mrs. Stone (WB, 1961)
Ship of Fools (Col., 1965)

Carole Lombard
(1908–1942)

Carole Lombard was born in Fort Wayne, Indiana. Her parents divorced and she moved to California at an early age with her mother and brothers. She got her first screen role at the age of 12. After graduation from high school she went to drama school and received a contract from Fox. When her contract expired she was signed by Mack Sennett and appeared in slapstick comedies. She returned to feature films under the Paramount banner, appearing in routine films at her home studio and on loan-outs. She married William Powell and after two years of marriage they divorced. In 1934 she became a top comedy star in "Twentieth Century" while on loan to Columbia. It was directed by Howard Hawk and co-starred John Barrymore. Her popularity continued under top directors Gregory LaCava, William Wellman, Ernst Lubitsch, Mitchell Leisen and Alfred Hitchcock. She married Clark Gable in 1939. Returning from Indianapolis during a war bond tour in January 1941, she was killed in a plane crash.

Top: Comedy, action and romance are blended in *No Man of Her Own* in which Clark Gable and Carole Lombard appeared together for the first time. This union resulted in their happy marriage several years later (Paramount, 1932). *Bottom:* James Stewart is the struggling young attorney and Carole Lombard (holding Jackie Taylor) is his wife in the dramatic film *Made for Each Other* (United Artists, 1939).

Carole Lombard Sound Feature Films (1928–1942)

Show Folks (Pathé, 1928)
Ned McCobb's Daughter (Pathé, 1929)
High Voltage (Pathé, 1929)
Big News (Pathé, 1929)
Dynamite (Pathé, 1929)
The Racketeer (Pathé, 1929)
Arizona Kid (Fox, 1930)
Safety in Numbers (Par., 1930)
Fast and Loose (Par., 1930)
It Pays to Advertise (Par., 1931)
Man of the World (Par., 1931)
Ladies' Man (Par., 1931)
Up Pops the Devil (Par., 1931)
I Take This Woman (Par., 1931)
No One Man (Par., 1932)
Sinners in the Sun (Par., 1932)
Virtue (Col., 1932)
No More Orchids (Col., 1932)
No Man of Her Own (Par., 1932)
From Hell to Heaven (Par., 1933)
Supernatural (Par., 1933)
The Eagle and the Hawk (Par., 1933)
Brief Moment (Col., 1933)
White Woman (Par., 1933)

Bolero (Par., 1934)
We're Not Dressing (Par., 1934)
Twentieth Century (Col., 1934)
Now and Forever (Par., 1934)
Lady by Choice (Col., 1934)
The Gay Bride (MGM, 1934)
Rumba (Par., 1935)
Hands Across the Table (Par., 1935)
Love Before Breakfast (Univ., 1936)
My Man Godfrey (Univ., 1936)
The Princess Comes Across (Par., 1936)
Swing High, Swing Low (Par., 1937)
True Confession (Par., 1937)
Nothing Sacred (UA, 1937)
Fools for Scandal (WB, 1938)
Made for Each Other (UA, 1939)
In Name Only (RKO, 1939)
Vigil in the Night (RKO, 1940)
They Knew What They Wanted (RKO, 1940)
Mr. and Mrs. Smith (RKO, 1941)
To Be or Not to Be (UA, 1942)

Hattie McDaniel
(1895–1952)

Hattie McDaniel was born in Wichita, Kansas. Her father was a preacher and her mother a spiritual singer. At the age of 15 she won a drama contest. She began her professional career as a singer in a band and was the first black woman to sing on radio. In her film debut, *The Golden West* (Fox), she played a maid. Later she worked for all the major studios in Hollywood. On radio she appeared in *Amos and Andy, The Eddie Cantor Show* and *Beulah,* which was also done for television. In

Hattie McDaniel *(left)* and other players in *Maryland* helped insure the success of the film (20th Century–Fox, 1940).

1939 she won an Oscar for the best supporting actress for her performance as Mammy in *Gone with the Wind.*

Hattie McDaniel Feature Films (1932–1948)

The Golden West (Fox, 1932)
Blonde Venus (Par., 1932)
Hypnotized (World Wide, 1932)
Washington Masquerade (MGM, 1932)
I'm No Angel (Par., 1933)
The Story of Temple Drake (Par., 1933)
Operator 13 (MGM, 1934)
Judge Priest (Fox, 1934)
Lost in the Stratosphere (Mon., 1934)
Babbitt (WB, 1934)
Little Men (RKO, 1934)
Imitation of Life (Univ., 1934)
The Little Colonel (Fox, 1935)
Alice Adams (RKO, 1935)
Music Is Magic (20th, 1935)
Another Face (RKO, 1935)
Traveling Saleslady (WB, 1935)
Next Time We Love (Univ., 1936)
Libeled Lady (MGM, 1936)
Gentle Julia (20th, 1936)

Vivien Leigh as Scarlet O'Hara dons her best dress with the help of Mammy (Hattie McDaniel) to attend the barbecue in *Gone with the Wind* (MGM, 1939).

The First Baby (20th, 1936)
Show Boat (Univ., 1936)
Hearts Divided (WB, 1936)
High Treason (20th, 1936)
Star for a Night (20th, 1936)
The Postal Inspector (Univ., 1936)
The Bride Walks Out (RKO, 1936)
The Singing Kid (WB, 1936)
Valiant Is the Word for Carrie (Par., 1936)
Reunion (20th, 1936)
Can This Be Dixie? (20th, 1936)
Racing Lady (RKO, 1937)
Don't Tell the Wife (RKO, 1937)
The Crime Nobody Saw (Par., 1937)

Saratoga (MGM, 1937)
Merry-Go-Round of 1938 (Univ., 1937)
True Confession (Par., 1937)
The Wildcatter (Univ., 1937)
45 Fathers (Univ., 1937)
Over the Goal (WB, 1937)
Nothing Sacred (UA, 1937)
Battle of Broadway (20th, 1938)
The Shopworn Angel (MGM, 1938)
Carefree (RKO, 1938)
The Shining Hour (MGM, 1938)
The Mad Miss Manton (RKO, 1938)
Everybody's Baby (20th, 1939)
Zenobia (UA, 1939)

Gone with the Wind (MGM, 1939)
Maryland (20th, 1940)
The Great Lie (WB, 1941)
Affectionately Yours (WB, 1941)
They Died with Their Boots On (WB, 1941)
The Male Animal (WB, 1942)
This Is Our Life (WB, 1942)
George Washington Slept Here (WB, 1942)
Reap the Wild Wind (Par., 1942)
Johnny Come Lately (UA, 1943)
Thank Your Lucky Stars (WB, 1943)

Janie (WB, 1944)
Since You Went Away (UA, 1944)
Three Is a Family (UA, 1944)
Hi, Beautiful (Univ., 1945)
Janie Gets Married (WB, 1946)
Margie (20th, 1946)
Song of the South (RKO, 1946)
Never Say Goodbye (WB, 1946)
The Flame (Rep., 1947)
Mickey (EL, 1948)
Mr. Blandings Builds His Dream House (RKO, 1948)
Family Honeymoon (Univ., 1948)

Jeanette MacDonald
(1901–1965)

Jeanette MacDonald was born in Philadelphia and made her New York debut in 1920 in the chorus of a musical. The Shuberts saw her and signed her to a contract. She starred in many of their hit musicals and operettas on Broadway and on tour. Richard Dix persuaded Paramount to test her. Ernst Lubitsch saw the test and cast her opposite Maurice Chevalier in *The Love Parade*.

After her brief contract with Paramount, she did three films for Fox and one for United Artists. She made a successful concert tour of Europe and returned to Paramount to do two films under Lubitsch. She next signed with MGM and did *The Cat and the Fiddle* opposite Ramon Navarro and *The Merry Widow* opposite Maurice Chevalier under Lubitsch's direction. She was then co-starred with an unknown singer, Nelson Eddy, in *Naughty Marietta*. It was an international success. They were reunited many times and were known as *America's Singing Sweethearts*.

In 1937 Jeanette MacDonald married actor Gene Raymond. She appeared opposite Ezio Pinza in grand opera in *Romeo and Juliet* and *Faust*. She returned to films occasionally, did concert work and played in stock and musicals until her death in 1965.

Jeanette MacDonald *(center)* as *Naughty Marietta,* a French princess who flees in disguise to New Orleans and informs Frank Morgan (the governor) and his wife (Elsa Lanchester) that she is not interested in marrying any colonist (MGM, 1935).

Jeanette MacDonald Feature Films (1929–1948)

The Love Parade (Par., 1929)
The Vagabond King (Par., 1930)
Monte Carlo (Par., 1930)
Let's Go Native (Par., 1930)
The Lottery Bride (UA, 1930)
Oh, for a Man (Fox, 1930)
Don't Bet on Women (Fox, 1931)
Annabelle's Affairs (Fox, 1931)

One Hour with You (Par., 1932)
Love Me Tonight (Par., 1932)
The Cat and the Fiddle (MGM, 1934)
The Merry Widow (MGM, 1934)
Naughty Marietta (MGM, 1935)
Rose Marie (MGM, 1936)
San Francisco (MGM, 1936)

Nelson Eddy is the singing teacher who runs off to marry Jeanette MacDonald. They become street singers in Vienna in *Bitter Sweet*, based on a Noel Coward operetta (MGM, 1940).

Maytime (MGM, 1937)
The Firefly (MGM, 1937)
The Girl of the Golden West (MGM, 1938)
Sweethearts (MGM, 1938)
Broadway Serenade (MGM, 1939)
New Moon (MGM, 1940)
Bitter Sweet (MGM, 1940)

Smilin' Through (MGM, 1941)
I Married an Angel (MGM, 1942)
Cairo (MGM, 1942)
Follow the Boys (Univ., 1944)
Three Daring Daughters (MGM, 1948)
The Sum Comes Up (MGM, 1948)

Victor McLaglen
(1886–1959)

Victor McLaglen, the oldest of eight brothers, was born in Tunbridge Wells, England. His father was a clergyman. He was a soldier during the Boer War, then went to Canada where he worked on farms. McLaglen became a prizefighter and then a circus performer. This led to vaudeville and tours of the United States and Australia. With the outbreak of World War I in 1914 he returned to England, joined the Irish Fusiliers, and served in the Middle East. At the end of the war he returned to boxing. Producer I.B. Davidson signed him to appear in films. He was a success in his first film and became a top British film actor. Soon he had Hollywood offers and accepted work at all the top studios before signing with Fox. He made a successful transition from silent films to talkies under the direction of John Ford. In 1935 Ford and McLaglen were united again in *The Informer*. It won four Academy Awards for best actor, best director, best screenplay and best musical score. He continued to appear with many top stars until his death in 1959.

Victor McLaglen Sound Feature Films (1929–1957)

Black Watch (Fox, 1929)
Cock-Eyed World (Fox, 1929)
Hot for Paris (Fox, 1929)
Happy Days (Fox, 1930)
On the Level (Fox, 1930)
Devil with Women (Fox, 1930)
Dishonored (Par., 1931)
Not Exactly Gentlemen (Fox, 1931)
Annabelle's Affairs (Fox, 1931)
Women of All Nations (Fox, 1931)
Wicked (Fox, 1931)
The Gay Caballero (Fox, 1932)
Devil's Lottery (Fox, 1932)
While Paris Sleeps (Fox, 1932)
Guilty as Hell (Par., 1932)
Rackety Rax (Fox, 1932)
Dick Turpin (GB, 1933)
Hot Pepper (Fox, 1933)
Laughing at Life (Mascot, 1933)
No More Women (Par., 1934)
The Lost Patrol (RKO, 1934)
Wharf Angel (Par., 1934)

Murder at the Vanities (Par., 1934)
The Captain Hates the Sea (Col., 1934)
Under Pressure (Fox, 1935)
Great Hotel Murder (Fox, 1935)
The Informer (RKO, 1935)
Professional Soldier (Fox, 1935)
Klondike Annie (Par., 1936)
Under Two Flags (20th, 1936)
Mary of Scotland (RKO, 1936)
The Magnificent Brute (Univ., 1936)
Sea Devils (RKO, 1937)
Nancy Steele Is Missing (20th, 1937)
This Is My Affair (20th, 1937)
Wee Willie Winkie (20th, 1937)
Battle of Broadway (20th, 1938)
The Devil's Party (Univ., 1938)
We're Going to Be Rich (20th, 1938)
Pacific Liner (RKO, 1939)
Let Freedom Ring (MGM, 1939)

Top: Victor McLaglen *(left)* and Edmund Lowe are two feuding deep-sea divers in *No More Women* (Paramount, 1934). *Bottom:* C. Aubrey Smith *(left)* is a colonel and Victor McLaglen is a sergeant at a British outpost in India in *Wee Willie Winkie,* based on a Rudyard Kipling story (20th Century–Fox, 1937).

Captain Fury (UA, 1939)
Ex-Champ (Univ., 1939)
Full Confession (RKO, 1939)
Rio (Univ., 1939)
The Big Guy (Univ., 1939)
Diamond Frontier (Univ., 1940)
Broadway Limited (UA, 1941)
Call Out the Marines (RKO, 1942)
Powder Town (RKO, 1942)
China Girl (20th, 1942)
Forever and a Day (RKO, 1943)
Tampico (20th, 1944)
Roger Tuohy, Gangster (20th, 1944)
The Princess and the Pirate (RKO, 1944)
Rough, Tough and Ready (RKO, 1945)
Love, Honor and Goodbye
(Rep., 1945)
Whistle Stop (UA, 1946)
Calendar Girl (Rep., 1947)
The Michigan Kid (Univ., 1947)
The Foxes of Harrow (20th, 1947)
Fort Apache (RKO, 1948)
She Wore a Yellow Ribbon (RKO, 1949)
Rio Grande (Rep., 1950)
The Quiet Man (Rep., 1952)
Fair Wind to Java (Rep., 1953)
Prince Valiant (20th, 1954)
Trouble in the Glen (Rep., 1954)
Many Rivers to Cross (MGM, 1955)
City of Shadows (Rep., 1955)
Bengazi (RKO, 1955)
Lady Godiva (Univ., 1955)
The Abductors (20th, 1957)

Fredric March
(1897–1975)

Fredric March was born in Racine, Wisconsin. He studied at the state university and was headed for a banking career but changed his mind and decided to become an actor. In New York he obtained jobs as a model and an extra in silent films. He made his Broadway debut in *Deburau*. This led to other Broadway hits in which he toured. While playing in *The Royal Family* in California he was signed to a Paramount contract. With that studio he appeared opposite Ruth Chatterton, Clara Bow, Ann Harding, Jeanne Eagels, Colleen Moore, Mary Astor, Nancy Carroll, Claudette Colbert and Tallulah Bankhead. In 1927 he married actress Florence Eldridge and their union lasted 48 years. He won his first Oscar in 1932 as the star of *Dr. Jekyll and Mr. Hyde*. With his wife he appeared in films and on the New York stage in such hits as *The American Way, Hopes for a Harvest, The Skin of Our Teeth* and *Years Ago*. He received his second Oscar for *The Best Years of Our Lives* in 1946. After appearing in many films he returned to Broadway in Eugene

The Sign of the Cross, **Cecil B. DeMille's spectacle of decadence in ancient Rome, cast Fredric March as the dashing Prefect of Rome and Claudette Colbert as Empress Poppaea, wife of Emperor Nero (Paramount, 1932).**

O'Neill's *Long Day's Journey into Night* opposite his wife. For this performance he won the Critic's Best Actor Award. In 1954 he did *The Royal Family* for television opposite Claudette Colbert and Helen Hayes. After a 40-year career, he was still appearing on the stage and screen until shortly before his death of cancer in 1975.

Fredric March Feature Films (1929–1973)

The Dummy (Par., 1929)
The Wild Party (Par., 1929)
The Studio Murder Mystery

(Par., 1929)
Paris Bound (Par., 1929)
Footlights and Fools (WB, 1929)

Fredric March as Willy Loman is fired from his job with nowhere to go at age 60. Mildred Dunnock plays his long-suffering wife in *Death of a Salesman* (Columbia, 1951).

The Marriage Playground (Par., 1929)
Sarah and Son (Par., 1930)
Ladies Love Brutes (Par., 1930)
Paramount on Parade (Par., 1930)
True to the Navy (Par., 1930)
Manslaughter (Par., 1930)
Laughter (Par., 1930)
Honor Among Lovers (Par., 1931)
The Night Angel (Par., 1931)
My Sin (Par., 1931)
Dr. Jekyll and Mr. Hyde (Par., 1931)
Strangers in Love (Par., 1932)
Merrily We Go to Hell (Par., 1932)

Make Me a Star (Par., 1932)
Smilin' Through (MGM, 1932)
The Sign of the Cross (Par., 1932)
Tonight Is Ours (Par., 1933)
The Eagle and the Hawk (Par., 1933)
Design for Living (Par., 1933)
All of Me (Par., 1934)
Death Takes a Holiday (Par., 1934)
Good Dame (Par., 1934)
The Affairs of Cellini (UA, 1934)
The Barretts of Wimpole Street (MGM, 1934)
We Live Again (UA, 1934)
Les Miserables (UA, 1935)
Anna Karenina (MGM, 1935)

The Dark Angel (UA, 1935)
Anthony Adverse (WB, 1936)
The Road to Glory (20th, 1936)
Mary of Scotland (RKO, 1936)
A Star Is Born (UA, 1937)
Nothing Sacred (UA, 1937)
The Buccaneer (Par., 1938)
There Goes My Heart (UA, 1938)
Trade Winds (UA, 1938)
Susan and God (MGM, 1940)
Victory (Par., 1940)
So Ends Our Night (UA, 1941)
One Foot in Heaven (WB, 1941)
Bedtime Story (Col., 1941)
I Married a Witch (UA, 1942)
The Adventures of Mark Twain (WB, 1944)
Tomorrow the World (UA, 1944)
The Best Years of Our Lives (RKO, 1946)
Another Part of the Forest (Univ., 1948)
Live Today for Tomorrow (Univ., 1948)
Christopher Columbus (Rank, 1949)
It's a Big Country (MGM, 1951)
Death of a Salesman (Col., 1951)
Man on a Tightrope (20th, 1953)
Executive Suite (MGM, 1954)
The Bridges at Toko-Ri (Par., 1954)
The Desperate Hours (Par., 1955)
Alexander the Great (UA, 1956)
The Man in the Gray Flannel Suit (20th, 1956)
Albert Schweitzer (narrator; Derochemont, 1957)
Middle of the Night (Col., 1959)
The Condemned of Altona (20th, 1963)
Seven Days in May (Par., 1964)
Hombre (20th, 1967)
Tick, Tick, Tick (MGM, 1970)
The Iceman Cometh (AFT, 1973)

The Marx Brothers

Chico (1891–1961)   Harpo (1893–1964)
Groucho (1895–1977)   Zeppo (1901–   )

The Marx Brothers were born in New York of German-Jewish descent. The boys' mother, sister of vaudeville star Al Sheean, pushed her sons into show business at an early age. By 1914 they were touring in vaudeville under the billing *The Greatest Comedy Act in Show Business*. Their first book show, *I'll Say She Is*, toured the country for two years before opening on Broadway in 1924 to excellent reviews. Next came *The Cocoanuts* in 1925 and *Animal Crackers* in 1928. Paramount signed them to a contract and they appeared in five successful films. In 1935 Irving Thalberg signed them for Metro-Goldwyn-Mayer and they made two great successes before Thalberg's death. They made three more

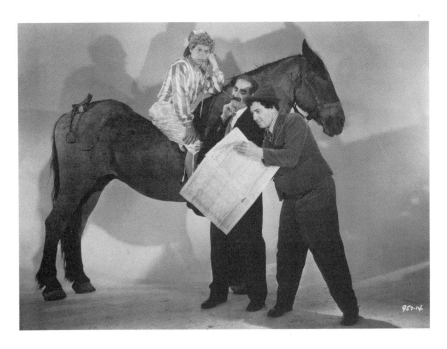

Groucho Marx *(center)* is a horse doctor who takes over a santarium. His brothers Harpo *(on horse)* and Chico are his sidekicks in *A Day at the Races* (MGM, 1937).

films under their contract at MGM and one at RKO. The brothers did two more films together which were released by United Artists before the team broke up. Chico played vaudeville independently and had his own band. Groucho turned to writing. He wrote screenplays, a play with Norman Krasna entitled *A Time for Elizabeth,* and four successful books: *Beds, Many Happy Returns, Groucho and Me* and *The Groucho Letters.* He appeared in several films and had a 14-year run on NBC's radio and television show *You Bet Your Life.* Groucho also did a one-man show at Carnegie Hall. He toured briefly in it before it closed because of his ill health.

Marx Brothers Sound Feature Films: (1929–1968)

With Chico, Harpo, Groucho, Zeppo

The Cocoanuts (Par., 1929)
Animal Crackers (Par., 1930)
Monkey Business (Par., 1931)
Horse Feathers (Par., 1932)
Duck Soup (Par., 1933)

With Chico, Harpo, Groucho

A *Night at the Opera* (MGM, 1935)

A *Day at the Races* (MGM, 1937)

Room Service (RKO, 1938)

At the Circus (MGM, 1939)

Go West (MGM, 1940)

The Big Store (MGM, 1941)

A *Night in Casablanca* (UA, 1946)

Love Happy (UA, 1950)

The Story of Mankind (WB, 1957)

With Harpo

Stage Door Canteen (UA, 1943)

With Groucho

Copacabana (UA, 1947)

Mr. Music (Par., 1950)

Double Dynamite (RKO, 1951)

A *Girl in Every Port* (RKO, 1952)

Will Success Spoil Rock Hunter? (unbilled guest appearance; 20th, 1957)

Skidoo (Par., 1968)

Marilyn Monroe
(1926–1962)

Born Norma Jean Mortenson in Los Angeles, she was brought up in orphanages and numerous foster homes. Her mother, a film cutter, was confined to mental institutions. At the age of 16 she quit high school for a marriage which was brief and ended in divorce. During World War II she worked in a defense plant. Then she became a photographer's model. This led to film contracts and changing her name to Marilyn Monroe. She first came to public attention when John Huston cast her in the MGM film *The Asphalt Jungle.* Twentieth Century–Fox groomed her for stardom by giving her acting and singing lessons and then casting her in important pictures. In 1954 she married baseball player Joe DiMaggio. The union ended in divorce after only one year. She briefly studied acting in New York at Actor's Studio, then met and married playwright Arthur Miller. They divorced after five years together.

Opposite: **Groucho Marx** *(in glasses)* **is a hotel manager in Florida during the land boom of the late 1920s with his brothers Harpo, Chico and Zeppo** *(from left to right)* **adding to the fun in** *The Cocoanuts.* **The tall man in the center is unidentified (Paramount, 1929).**

Top: Marilyn Monroe is a saloon singer and Robert Mitchum returns from prison during the gold rush days in northwest Canada in *River of No Return* (20th Century–Fox, 1954). *Bottom:* Marilyn Monroe complains about the heat as she stands over a subway grating. Her dress flies up from a blast of cool air from the grating as Tom Ewell looks on in *The Seven Year Itch* (20th Century–Fox, 1955).

Marilyn Monroe

During this period she sought psychiatric help and their film *The Misfits* failed. She returned to Hollywood and began a new film but was fired because of incessant tardiness. Less than a month later she died as a result of an overdose of barbituates.

Marilyn Monroe Feature Films (1947–1962)

Dangerous Years (20th, 1947)
Ladies of the Chorus (Col., 1948)

A Ticket to Tomahawk (20th, 1950)
The Asphalt Jungle (MGM, 1950)

All About Eve (20th, 1950)
Right Cross (MGM, 1950)
The Fireball (20th, 1950)
Hometown Story (MGM, 1951)
As Young as You Feel (20th, 1951)
Love Nest (20th, 1951)
Let's Make It Legal (20th, 1951)
Clash by Night (RKO, 1952)
We're Not Married (20th, 1952)
Don't Bother to Knock (20th, 1952)
Monkey Business (20th, 1952)
O. Henry's Full House (20th, 1952)
Niagara (20th, 1953)

Gentlemen Prefer Blondes (20th, 1953)
How to Marry a Millionaire (20th, 1953)
River of No Return (20th, 1954)
There's No Business Like Show Business (20th, 1954)
The Seven Year Itch (20th, 1955)
Bus Stop (20th, 1956)
The Prince and the Showgirl (WB, 1957)
Some Like It Hot (UA, 1959)
Let's Make Love (20th, 1960)
The Misfits (UA, 1961)
Something's Got to Give (uncompleted, 1962)

Robert Montgomery
(1904–1981)

After his father's death in 1920 Montgomery worked as a railroad mechanic and a deckhand on a tanker. He hoped to be a writer of short stories in New York but turned to acting in stock and then established himself on the Broadway stage. In 1929 he made a screen test for Samuel Goldwyn. That led to a Metro-Goldwyn-Mayer contract which lasted for many years. He was president of the Screen Actors Guild for four terms. Before the United States entered World War II he drove an ambulance in France. During the war he served as a naval officer in both the Atlantic and Pacific and was decorated for valor. After the war he turned to directing films and plays. He received a Tony for directing *The Desperate Hours* and was nominated twice for the Academy Award in acting.

From 1950 to 1957 he produced, hosted and sometimes starred in the television series *Robert Montgomery Presents*. He served as radio and television advisor to President Eisenhower. Before his death he was president of the Lincoln Center Repertory Theatre and an active member of The National Citizens Committee for Broadcasting.

Joan Crawford is a jewel thief and William Powell *(right)* is her accomplice. Robert Montgomery is a playboy who upsets their plans in *The Last of Mrs. Cheyney* (MGM, 1937).

Robert Montgomery Sound Feature Films (1929–1960)

So This Is College (MGM, 1929)
Untamed (MGM, 1929)
Three Live Ghosts (MGM, 1929)
Single Standard (MGM, 1929)
Their Own Desire (MGM, 1930)
Free and Easy (MGM, 1930)
The Divorcee (MGM, 1930)

Big House (MGM, 1930)
Our Blushing Brides (MGM, 1930)
Sins of the Children ("Richest Man in the World" MGM, 1930)
Love in the Rough (MGM, 1930)

Robert Montgomery *(center)* is a suspected killer. In order to prove himself innocent he must find the real killer in *Mystery of Mr. X* with Elizabeth Allan and Ralph Forbes (MGM, 1934).

War Nurse (MGM, 1930)
The Easiest Way (MGM, 1931)
Strangers May Kiss (MGM, 1931)
Inspiration (MGM, 1931)
Shipmates (MGM, 1931)
Man in Possession (MGM, 1931)
Private Lives (MGM, 1931)
Lovers Courageous (MGM, 1932)
But the Flesh Is Weak (MGM, 1932)
Letty Lynton (MGM, 1932)
Blondie of the Follies (MGM, 1932)
Faithless (MGM, 1932)
Hell Below (MGM, 1933)
Made on Broadway (MGM, 1933)
When Ladies Meet (MGM, 1933)
Night Flight (MGM, 1933)
Another Language (MGM, 1933)
Fugitive Lovers (MGM, 1934)
Riptide (MGM, 1934)
Mystery of Mr. X (MGM, 1934)
Hideout (MGM, 1934)
Forsaking All Others (MGM, 1935)
Vanessa, Her Love Story (MGM, 1935)
Biography of a Bachelor Girl (MGM, 1935)
No More Ladies (MGM, 1935)
Petticoat Fever (MGM, 1936)
Trouble for Two (MGM, 1936)
Piccadilly Jim (MGM, 1936)

The Last of Mrs. Cheyney (MGM, 1937)
Night Must Fall (MGM, 1937)
Ever Since Eve (WB, 1937)
Live, Love and Learn (MGM, 1937)
The First Hundred Years (MGM, 1938)
Yellow Jack (MGM, 1938)
Three Loves Has Nancy (MGM, 1938)
Fast and Loose (MGM, 1939)
The Earl of Chicago (MGM, 1940)
Haunted Honeymoon (MGM, 1940)
Rage in Heaven (MGM, 1941)
Mr. and Mrs. Smith (RKO, 1941)

Here Comes Mr. Jordan (Col., 1941)
Unfinished Business (Univ., 1941)
They Were Expendable (MGM, 1945)
Lady in the Lake (MGM, 1946)
Ride the Pink Horse (Univ., 1947)
The Saxon Charm (Univ., 1948)
The Secret Land (narrator; MGM, 1948)
June Bride (WB, 1948)
Once More, My Darling (Univ., 1949)
Eye Witness (EL, 1950)
The Gallant Hours (dir., prod., unbilled cameo appearance; UA, 1960)

Paul Muni
(1895–1967)

Born into a family of strolling players in Austria, he appeared on the stage with them until they emigrated to the United States when he was seven. He worked on the Yiddish stage and in 1918 he joined the Yiddish Art Theatre and toured the United States and Europe. He made his debut in the English-language theatre in 1926. After a few years he had established himself as an actor and secured a film contract with Fox. In his first picture he was nominated for an Oscar but made only two films and then returned to Broadway. He triumphed in Elmer Rice's *Counsellor-At-Law* an then returned to Hollywood in two very successful films, *Scarface* for Howard Hughes and *I Am a Fugitive from a Chain Gang* for Warners. For the latter he was nominated again for an Oscar but did not win. While under contract to Warner Brothers he won the Academy Award for *The Story of Louis Pasteur* and the New York Film Critics Award for *The Life of Emile Zola*. After another Broadway success in Maxwell Anderson's *Key Largo* he made films at other studios. In 1955 he scored a hit on Broadway in *Inherit the Wind*. More films followed, as well as a successful television performance on *Play-*

Howard Hughes produced *Scarface*, a story of gangsters (as depicted by George Raft *[left]*, Paul Muni and Osgood Perkins) with money, cars and women who thumb their noses at authority (United Artists, 1932).

house 90. He toured in the musical *At the Grand* as a song and dance man. After his last films for Columbia his health declined and he died of a heart ailment.

Paul Mini Feature Films (1929–1959)

The Valiant (Fox, 1929)
Seven Faces (Fox, 1929)
Scarface (UA, 1932)
I Am a Fugitive from a Chain Gang (WB, 1932)
The World Changes (WB, 1933)
Hi, Nellie! (WB, 1934)
Bordertown (WB, 1935)
Black Fury (WB, 1935)

Dr. Socrates (WB, 1935)
The Story of Louis Pasteur (WB, 1935)
The Good Earth (MGM, 1937)
The Woman I Love (RKO, 1937)
The Life of Emile Zola (WB, 1937)
Juarez (WB, 1939)

Luise Rainer and Paul Muni are cast as a Chinese couple who struggle to exist in *The Good Earth*, based on Pearl Buck's Pulitzer Prize–winning novel (MGM, 1937).

We Are Not Alone (WB, 1939)
Hudson's Bay (20th, 1940)
Commandos Strike at Dawn (Col., 1942)
Stage Door Canteen (UA, 1943)
A Song to Remember (Col., 1945)

Counter-Attack (Col., 1945)
Angel on My Shoulder (UA, 1946)
Stranger on the Prowl (UA, 1953)
The Last Angry Man (Col., 1959)

Merle Oberon
(1911–1979)

Merle Oberon

She was christened Estelle Merle O'Brien Thompson in Tasmania and educated in India. At the age of 17 she went to London and worked as a dance hostess at the Cafe dé Paris under the name of Quennie O'Brien. She also worked as a film extra. Alexander Korda noticed her and signed her to a five-year contract. In 1935 Korda sold a share of her contract to Samuel Goldwyn and she went to Hollywood. She alternated between making films for Goldwyn in Hollywood and Korda in London. She married Korda in 1939 and severed ties with him after their divorce in 1945. Her second husband was cinematographer Lucien Ballard. Their marriage lasted four years. In 1957 she married a wealthy Italian industrialist and lived in Mexico until her divorce in 1973. In her last film, *Interval,* filmed in Mexico, she was her own producer. She married Robert Wolders who appeared opposite her in her last film.

Merle Oberon Feature Films (1932–1973)

Service for Ladies (Par., 1932)
Dance of Witches (London Film

Productions, 1932)
Wedding Rehearsal (London

Michael Rennie and Merle Oberon are guests who are being blackmailed at the St. Gregory Hotel in New Orleans. *Hotel* is based on Arthur Hailey's novel of the same title (Warner Bros., 1967).

Film Productions, 1932)

The Private Life of Henry VIII (London Film Productions, 1933)

The Private Life of Don Juan (UA, 1934)

Thunder in the East ("The Battle"; Leon Garganoff, 1934)

Broken Battle (Olympic Pictures, 1934)

Men of Tomorrow (Mundus, 1935)

The Scarlet Pimpernel (UA, 1935)

Folies Bergère (UA, 1935)

The Dark Angel (UA, 1935)

These Three (UA, 1936)

Beloved Enemy (UA, 1936)

The Divorce of Lady X (UA, 1938)

The Cowboy and the Lady (UA, 1938)

Wuthering Heights (UA, 1939)

The Lion Has Wings (UA, 1940)

Over the Moon (UA, 1940)

Till We Meet Again (WB, 1940)

Affectionately Yours (WB, 1941)

That Uncertain Feeling (UA, 1941)

Forever and a Day (RKO, 1943)

Stage Door Canteen (UA, 1943)

First Comes Courage (Col., 1943)

The Lodger (20th, 1944)

Dark Waters (UA, 1944)

A Song to Remember (Col., 1945)

This Love of Ours (Univ., 1945)

A Night in Paradise (Univ., 1946)

Temptation (Univ., 1946)

Night Song (Univ., 1947)

Berlin Express (RKO, 1948)
Pardon My French (UA, 1951)
Affair in Monte Carlo (AA, 1953)
Desirée (20th, 1954)
Deep in My Heart (MGM, 1954)

The Price of Fear (Univ., 1956)
Of Love and Desire (20th, 1963)
The Oscar (Par., 1966)
Hotel (WB, 1967)
Interval (Ind., 1973)

Dick Powell
(1904–1963)

Madeleine Carroll pleads with Dick Powell to cut offensive material from his musical which she sees as a take-off on her in *On the Avenue* (20th Century–Fox, 1937).

Powell was born in Mountain View, Arkansas. Before making his film debut in 1932, he worked for a telephone company and as a band instrumentalist and singer. While appearing at a theater in Pittsburgh, he was seen by a Warner Brothers' talent scout, tested, and signed to a contract. After a few minor roles he was cast opposite Ruby Keeler

Dick Powell becomes a cadet at the Naval Academy to please his father but wants a career as a singer in *Shipmates Forever* with Ruby Keeler as his dancing sweetheart (Warner Bros., 1935).

in the all-star film success *42nd Street.* They became a favorite musical team and their seven musicals together were top box office films. He married Joan Blondell in 1936 and they divorced in 1945. After leaving Warner Brothers he signed with Paramount and did films for MGM, RKO, Columbia and Universal. He then married June Allyson. He turned to television in 1952 and guest starred with David Niven and Charles Boyer in the successful *Four Star Playhouse* series. Other hit television shows followed and he turned to film directing and producing. In 1963 he died of cancer.

Dick Powell Feature Films (1932–1954)

Blessed Event (WB, 1932)
Too Busy to Work (Fox, 1932)
The King's Vacation (WB, 1933)

Gold Diggers of 1933 (WB, 1933)
Footlight Parade (WB, 1933)

College Coach (WB, 1933)
Convention City (WB, 1933)
Dames (WB, 1934)
Wonder Bar (WB, 1934)
Twenty Million Sweethearts (WB, 1934)
Happiness Ahead (WB, 1934)
Flirtation Walk (WB, 1934)
Gold Diggers of 1935 (WB, 1935)
Page Miss Glory (WB, 1935)
Broadway Gondalier (WB, 1935)
A Midsummer Night's Dream (WB, 1935)
Shipmates Forever (WB, 1935)
Thanks a Million (Fox, 1935)
Colleen (WB, 1936)
Hearts Divided (WB, 1936)
Stage Struck (WB, 1936)
Gold Diggers of 1937 (WB, 1936)
On the Avenue (20th, 1937)
The Singing Marine (WB, 1937)
Varsity Show (WB, 1937)
Hollywood Hotel (WB, 1937)
Cowboy from Brooklyn (WB, 1938)
Hard to Get (WB, 1938)
Going Places (WB, 1938)
Naughty but Nice (WB, 1939)
Christmas in July (Par., 1940)

I Want a Divorce (Par., 1940)
Model Wife (Univ., 1941)
In the Navy (Univ., 1941)
Star-Spangled Rhythm (Par., 1942)
Happy Go Lucky (Par., 1942)
True to Life (Par., 1943)
Riding High (Par., 1943)
It Happened Tomorrow (UA, 1944)
Meet the People (MGM, 1944)
Murder, My Sweet (RKO, 1944)
Cornered (RKO, 1945)
Johnny O'Clock (Col., 1947)
To the Ends of the Earth (Col., 1948)
Pitfall (UA, 1948)
Station West (RKO, 1948)
Rogue's Regiment (Univ., 1948)
Mrs. Mike (UA, 1949)
The Reformer and the Redhead (MGM, 1950)
Right Cross (MGM, 1950)
Callaway Went Thataway (MGM, 1951)
Cry Danger (RKO, 1951)
The Tall Target (MGM, 1951)
You Never Can Tell (Univ., 1951)
The Bad and the Beautiful (MGM, 1952)
Susan Slept Here (RKO, 1954)

Eleanor Powell
(1912–1982)

Discovered by Gus Edwards in Atlantic City while on vacation at the age of 12, she was given a job at the Ambassador Hotel. She made her Broadway debut at 16 at the Ziegfeld Roof, then did a specialty with Jack Haley in the Broadway show *Follow Through*. This led to appearances with Paul Whiteman and Maurice Chevalier at Carnegie Hall. On Broadway she appeared in *Hot Cha, Vanities* and *George White*

Top: Eleanor Powell *(seated)* is rejected for a role in a musical and Una Merkle comforts her in *Broadway Melody of 1936* (MGM, 1935). *Bottom, left to right:* Aboard ship en route to *Honolulu* Robert Young falls in love with Eleanor Powell. Gracie Allen and George Burns add to the zany doings in this screwball musical (MGM, 1939).

Scandals before going to Hollywood. Metro-Goldwyn-Mayer signed her and her first film for them was the hit *Broadway Melody of 1936*. After retiring she made a successful comeback in 1961 with her nightclub act appearing in Las Vegas and New York. She gave a command performance in Monaco for Princess Grace and also appeared on television to critical acclaim.

Eleanor Powell Film Credits (1935–1950)

George White's Scandals (Fox, 1935)
Broadway Melody of 1936 (MGM, 1935)
Born to Dance (MGM, 1936)
Broadway Melody of 1938 (MGM, 1937)
Rosalie (MGM, 1937)
Honolulu (MGM, 1939)
Broadway Meldoy of 1940 (MGM, 1940)
Lady Be Good (MGM, 1941)
Ship Ahoy (MGM, 1942)
I Dood It (MGM, 1943)
Thousands Cheer (MGM, 1943)
Sensations of 1945 (UA, 1944)
The Duchess of Idaho (MGM, 1950)

William Powell
(1892–1984)

William Powell was born in Pittsburgh, Pennsylvania. When he was 15 his family moved to Kansas City. After attending the University of Kansas for a brief time he worked for the telephone company. A wealthy aunt left him money to move to New York where he attended the American Academy of Dramatic Arts. His first important stage role was in Bayard Veiller's play *Within the Law* which toured for two years. He married Eileen Wilson, a member of the cast, in 1915. They had one son in 1925 and were divorced in 1931. After many years in stock he returned to Broadway in three hit productions before making his screen debut with John Barrymore in *Sherlock Holmes*. He made 34 silent films

Opposite: Rosalie had a budget of two million dollars with thousands of extras dressed in expensive costumes and many dance numbers like this one with Eleanor Powell *(hand up)* and Ray Bolger *(sword)* (MGM, 1937).

William Powell

and a successful transition to the talkies while under contract to Paramount. There he met and married Carole Lombard in 1931 but they divorced in 1933. After his Paramount contract expired he moved to Warner Brothers where he stayed for three years before going to Metro-Goldwyn-Mayer in 1934. There he was a box office favorite, appeared opposite Myrna Loy in 14 films, and was nominated for the Oscar three times. He never won it but he did win the New York Film Critics Award twice. In 1940 he married actress Diana Lewis. He retired from films in 1955 and moved to Palm Springs, California, where he died in 1984 at 91.

William Powell Sound Feature Films (1929–1955)

Interference (Par., 1929)
The Canary Murder Case (Par., 1929)
The Greene Murder Case (Par., 1929)
Charming Sinners (Par., 1929)
Four Feathers (Par., 1929)
Pointed Heels (Par., 1929)
The Benson Murder Case (Par., 1930)
Paramount on Parade (Par., 1930)
Shadow of the Law (Par., 1930)
Behind the Makeup (Par., 1930)
Street of Chance (Par., 1930)
For the Defense (Par., 1930)
Man of the World (Par., 1931)

Ladies' Man (Par., 1931)
Road to Singapore (WB, 1931)
High Pressure (WB, 1932)
Jewel Robbery (WB, 1932)
One Way Passage (WB, 1932)
Lawyer Man (WB, 1932)
Double Harness (RKO, 1933)
Private Detective 62 (WB, 1933)
The Kennel Murder Case (WB, 1933)
Fashions of 1934 (WB, 1934)
The Key (WB, 1934)
Manhattan Melodrama (MGM, 1934)
The Thin Man (MGM, 1934)
Evelyn Prentice (MGM, 1934)
Reckless (MGM, 1935)

William Powell as *The Great Ziegfeld* learns of the stock market crash, in which he loses everything, as Reginald Owen listens (MGM, 1936).

Star of Midnight (RKO, 1935)
Escapade (MGM, 1935)
Rendezvous (MGM, 1935)
The Great Ziegfeld (MGM, 1936)
The Ex–Mrs. Bradford (RKO, 1936)
My Man Godfrey (Univ., 1936)
Libeled Lady (MGM, 1936)
After the Thin Man (MGM, 1936)
The Last of Mrs. Cheyney (MGM, 1937)
The Emperor's Candlesticks (MGM, 1937)
Double Wedding (MGM, 1937)
The Baroness and the Butler (20th, 1938)

Another Thin Man (MGM, 1939)
I Love You Again (MGM, 1940)
Love Crazy (MGM, 1941)
Shadow of the Thin Man (MGM, 1941)
Crossroads (MGM, 1942)
The Youngest Profession (MGM, 1943)
The Heavenly Body (MGM, 1944)
The Thin Man Goes Home (MGM, 1944)
Ziegfeld Follies (MGM, 1946)
The Hoodlum Saint (MGM, 1946)
Song of the Thin Man (MGM, 1947)
Life with Father (WB, 1947)

The Senator Was Indiscreet
(Univ., 1947)
Mr. Peabody and the Mermaid
(Univ., 1948)
Take One False Step (Univ.,
1949)
Dancing in the Dark (20th,
1949)

The Treasure of Lost Canyon
(Univ., 1951)
It's a Big Country (MGM, 1951)
The Girl Who Had Everything
(MGM, 1953)
How to Marry a Millionaire
(20th, 1953)
Mister Roberts (WB, 1955)

Tyrone Power
(1913–1958)

Born in Cincinnati, Ohio, Tyrone Power was the son of a stage matinee idol who appeared in silent films and one talkie before his death in 1931. The younger Power did radio work and gained stage experience at an early age in Chicago. His first experience in Hollywood was disappointing so he went to New York. He joined Katharine Cornell's acting company where a talent scout from 20th Century saw him. After a successful screen test, he was cast in small but important roles by Darryl F. Zanuck before appearing in *Lloyds of London.* His role in that film made him a star.

Power continued as a major box office star at 20th Century until his service in the U.S. Marines during World War II. After the war he returned briefly to the theatre, first playing in stock opposite his first wife, Annabella. His film career continued at 20th Century but he was unhappy with his films even though they were successful at the box office. He returned to the stage in London as the lead in the hit *Mister Roberts.*

After his studio contract expired, he was in Charles Laughton's theatrical reading *John Brown's Body* and then did films of his choice at 20th Century and other studios. He was a great success in the film of Agatha Christie's *Witness for the Prosecution* and then toured the United States with Faye Emerson in the abridged version of *Back to Methuselah.*

Tyrone Power died in Spain while making a film under the direction of King Vidor.

Agatha Christie's *Witness for the Prosecution* is brought to the screen by Billy Wilder. Tyrone Power is on trial for murder (United Artists, 1957).

Tyrone Power Feature Films (1932–1957)

Tom Brown of Culver (Univ., 1932)

Flirtation Walk (WB, 1934)

Girls' Dormitory (20th, 1936)

Ladies in Love (20th, 1936)

Lloyds of London (20th, 1937)

Love Is News (20th, 1937)

Cafe Metropole (20th, 1937)

Thin Ice (20th, 1937)

Second Honeymoon (20th, 1937)

In Old Chicago (20th, 1938)

Alexander's Ragtime Band (20th, 1938)

Marie Antoinette (MGM, 1938)

Suez (20th, 1938)

Jesse James (20th, 1939)

Rose of Washington Square (20th, 1939)

Second Fiddle (20th, 1939)

The Rains Came (20th, 1939)

Daytime Wife (20th, 1939)

Johnny Apollo (20th, 1940)

Brigham Young—Frontiersman (20th, 1940)

The Return of Frank James (20th, 1940)

Mark of Zorro (20th, 1940)

Blood and Sand (20th, 1941)

A Yank in the R.A.F. (20th, 1941)

Son of Fury (20th, 1942)

This Above All (20th, 1942)

The Black Swan (20th, 1942)

Crash Dive (20th, 1943)

The Razor's Edge (20th, 1946)

Nightmare Alley (20th, 1947)

Captain from Castile (20th, 1947)

Luck of the Irish (20th, 1948)

Ernest Hemingway's *The Sun Also Rises* cast Tyrone Power as Jake Barnes, an American expatriate drifting in Europe, and Ava Gardner as Lady Brett Ashley (20th Century–Fox, 1957).

That Wonderful Urge (20th, 1948)
Prince of Foxes (20th, 1949)
The Black Rose (20th, 1950)
An American Guerrilla in the Philippines (20th, 1950)
Rawhide (20th, 1951)
I'll Never Forget You (20th, 1951)
Diplomatic Courier (20th, 1952)
Pony Soldier (20th, 1952)
Mississippi Gambler (Univ., 1953)

King of the Khyber Rifles (20th, 1953)
The Long Gray Line (Col., 1955)
Untamed (20th, 1955)
The Eddy Duchin Story (Col., 1956)
Abandon Ship (Col., 1957)
The Rising of the Moon (WB, 1957)
The Sun Also Rises (20th, 1957)
Witness for the Prosecution (UA, 1957)

Elvis Presley
(1935–1977)

Elvis Presley was born in Tupelo, Mississippi, to Vernon and Gladys Presley. His twin brother Jessie died at birth. He had his first

Elvis Presley

singing experiences in the choir of a local church and later at revivals and camp meetings. He won fifth prize in a radio amateur singing contest. At the age of 12 he received a guitar for a birthday present and taught himself to play it by listening to phonograph records. In 1949 the family moved to Memphis, Tennessee, where Elvis graduated from L.C. Humes High School in 1953. After graduation he became a truck driver and studied at night to be an electrician. He went to Sun Record Company to cut a personal record as a present to his mother. Sam Phillips, president of the company, signed Elvis to a recording contract. Colonel Thomas A. Parker became Elvis' personal manager and in 1956 he became a show business phenomenon, enjoying a huge success in

Top: Elvis Presley *(right)* plays a pilot who goes to the 1962 Seattle World's Fair and falls in love. Gary Lockwood is his sidekick in *It Happened at the World's Fair* (MGM, 1963). *Bottom:* Elvis Presley's first screen appearance was in *Love Me Tender* (with Debra Paget), a routine western taking place at the end of the Civil War. It was highlighted by Elvis' singing (20th Century–Fox, 1956).

television, records and films. In 1958 Presley was inducted into the army and assigned to a tour of duty in Germany. He was discharged in 1961 and returned to a successful career, adding appearances in Las Vegas. He married Pricilla Beaulieu in 1967 and a daughter, Lisa Marie, was born in 1968. His immense popularity continued under the guidance of Colonel Parker. He died in Memphis of heart failure in 1977.

Elvis Presley Feature Films (1956–1972)

Love Me Tender (20th, 1956)
Loving You (Par., 1957)
Jailhouse Rock (MGM, 1957)
King Creole (Par., 1958)
G.I. Blues (Par., 1960)
Flaming Stars (20th, 1960)
Wild in the Country (20th, 1961)
Blue Hawaii (Par., 1961)
Kid Galahad (UA, 1962)
Girls! Girls! Girls! (Par., 1962)
Fun in Acapulco (Par., 1963)
It Happened at the World's Fair (MGM, 1963)
Kissin' Cousins (MGM, 1964)
Viva Las Vegas (MGM, 1964)
Roustabout (Par., 1964)
Girl Happy (MGM, 1965)
Tickle Me (AA, 1965)
Harum Scarum (MGM, 1965)
Frankie and Johnny (UA, 1966)
Paradise—Hawaiian Style (Par., 1966)
Spinout (MGM, 1966)
Easy Come, Easy Go (Par., 1967)
Double Trouble (MGM, 1967)
Speedway (MGM, 1968)
Stay Away, Joe (MGM, 1968)
Clambake (MGM, 1968)
Live a Little, Love a Little (MGM, 1968)
Charro (NGP, 1969)
The Trouble with Girls (MGM, 1969)
Change of Habit (Univ., 1969)
That's the Way It Is (doc.; MGM, 1970)
Elvis on Tour (doc.; MGM, 1972)

Claude Rains
(1889–1967)

Claude Rains was born in South London. At the age of ten he made his stage debut. After playing small roles and working backstage he became an assistant stage manager. He served in the British army (1915–1917) during World War I. After his discharge he made a name for

Philip Dorn *(left)* **is an army deserter from French Guiana who is picked up by a French freighter and questioned by Claude Rains** *(right)* **in** *Passage to Marseille* **(Warner Bros., 1944).**

himself on the London stage in numerous hit plays. He then came to the United States and became a Broadway star. Director James Whale saw a test he made at RKO and signed him for the lead in *Invisible Man*. He made several other films before signing a long-term contract with Warner Brothers. He was nominated four times for an Oscar but he never won. In 1947 his contract with Warner Brothers ended and he free-lanced at various studios. In 1950 he returned to Broadway in the successful *Darkness at Noon*. He toured in stock thereafter, appeared occasionally in films, and made another return to Broadway in T.S. Eliot's *The Confidential Clerk*. He was known as a brilliant supporting actor and appeared on the stage until his death in 1967.

Claude Rains Feature Films (1933–1965)

The Invisible Man (Univ., 1933)

Crime Without Passion (Par., 1934)

Alfred Hitchcock combined romance and suspense with mystery and action. Claude Rains *(center, facing camera)* **and Ingrid Bergman** *(left)* **are with two guests at a party in** *Notorious* **(RKO, 1946).**

The Man Who Reclaimed His Head (Univ., 1935)
The Clairvoyant (GB, 1935)
The Mystery of Edwin Drood (Univ., 1935)
The Last Outpost (Par., 1935)
Anthony Adverse (WB, 1936)
Hearts Divided (WB, 1936)
Stolen Holiday (WB, 1936)
The Prince and the Pauper (WB, 1937)
They Won't Forget (WB, 1937)
Gold Is Where You Find It (WB, 1938)
The Adventures of Robin Hood (WB, 1938)
White Banners (WB, 1938)
Four Daughters (WB, 1938)

They Made Me a Criminal (WB, 1939)
Juarez (WB, 1939)
Daughters Courageous (WB, 1939)
Mr. Smith Goes to Washington (Col., 1939)
Four Wives (WB, 1939)
Saturday's Children (WB, 1940)
The Sea Hawk (WB, 1940)
The Lady with Red Hair (WB, 1940)
Four Mothers (WB, 1941)
Here Comes Mr. Jordan (Col., 1941)
The Wolf Man (Univ., 1941)
King's Row (WB, 1941)
Moontide (20th, 1942)

Now, Voyager (WB, 1942)
Casablanca (WB, 1942)
The Phantom of the Opera (Univ., 1943)
Forever and a Day (RKO, 1943)
Passage to Marseille (WB, 1944)
Mr. Skeffington (WB, 1944)
This Love of Ours (Univ., 1945)
Angel on My Shoulder (UA, 1946)
Caesar and Cleopatra (UA, 1946)
Strange Holiday (PRC, 1946)
Notorious (RKO, 1946)
Deception (WB, 1946)
The Unsuspected (WB, 1947)

One Woman's Story (Univ., 1949)
Rope of Sand (Par., 1949)
Song of Surrender (Par., 1949)
The White Tower (RKO, 1950)
Where Danger Lies (RKO, 1950)
Sealed Cargo (RKO, 1951)
The Paris Express (George J. Schaeffer, 1953)
Lisbon (Rep., 1956)
This Earth Is Mine (Univ., 1959)
The Lost World (20th, 1960)
Lawrence of Arabia (Col., 1962)
Twilight of Honor (MGM, 1963)
The Greatest Story Ever Told (UA, 1965)

Edward G. Robinson
(1893–1973)

Edward Robinson was born Emanuel Goldenberg in Bucharest, Rumania, in 1893 and came to the United States at the age of ten with his parents and four brothers. They settled on the lower east side of New York. He studied at New York City College and Columbia University, graduated with honors from Columbia and went on to obtain a Master of Arts degree. In 1912 he attended the American Academy of Dramatic Arts and then toured in stock companies and made his Broadway debut in *Under Fire* (1915). He appeared in ten plays for the Theatre Guild, a vaudeville act and a play he wrote himself.

After serving in the navy in World War I he returned to Broadway in *The Last Is First*. His first film was *The Bright Shawl* with Dorothy Gish. His first sound film was produced in 1929 and in 1931 he scored an outstanding success in *Little Caesar* which made him a star. For many years he was a Hollywood favorite. He won the best actor award at the Cannes film festival in 1949 for his role in *The House of Strangers*. In 1956 he returned in triumph to Broadway in Paddy Chayefsky's *Middle of the Night*.

Little Caesar was the film which launched the gangster movie cycle. Edward G. Robinson with his hoodlums takes over a nightclub (Warner Bros., 1930).

After a heart attack in 1962 his movie-making pace slowed down. He was awarded the first honorary award recognizing lifetime contributions to motion pictures but he died before the awards night presentation.

Edward G. Robinson Sound Film Credits (1929–1973)

The Hole in the Wall (Par., 1929)
Night Ride (Univ., 1930)
A Lady to Love (MGM, 1930)
Outside the Law (Univ., 1930)
East Is West (Univ., 1930)
The Widow from Chicago (WB, 1930)
Little Caesar (WB, 1930)
Smart Money (WB, 1931)
Five Star Final (WB, 1931)
The Hatchet Man (WB, 1932)

Two Seconds (WB, 1932)
Tiger Shark (WB, 1932)
Silver Dollar (WB, 1932)
Little Giant (WB, 1933)
I Loved a Woman (WB, 1933)
Dark Hazard (WB, 1934)
The Man with Two Faces (WB, 1934)
The Whole Town's Talking (Col., 1935)
Barbary Coast (UA, 1935)
Bullets or Ballots (WB, 1936)

Frank Craven *(left)*, editor of a newspaper, and his employees are threatened by Edward G. Robinson, crime lord of the *Barbary Coast* (United Artists, 1935).

Thunder in the City (Col., 1937)
Kid Galahad (WB, 1937)
The Last Gangster (MGM, 1937)
A Slight Case of Murder (WB, 1938)
The Amazing Dr. Clitterhouse (WB, 1938)
I Am the Law (Col., 1938)
Confessions of a Nazi Spy (WB, 1939)
Blackmail (MGM, 1939)
Dr. Ehrlich's Magic Bullet (WB, 1940)
Brother Orchid (WB, 1940)
A Dispatch from Reuters (WB, 1940)
The Sea Wolf (WB, 1941)
Manpower (WB, 1941)
Larceny, Inc. (WB, 1942)

Tales of Manhattan (20th, 1942)
Destroyer (Col., 1943)
Flesh and Fantasy (Univ., 1943)
Tampico (20th, 1944)
Double Indemnity (Par., 1944)
Mr. Winkle Goes to War (Col., 1944)
The Woman in the Window (RKO, 1944)
Our Vines Have Tender Grapes (MGM, 1945)
Scarlet Street (Univ., 1945)
The Stranger (RKO, 1946)
The Red House (UA, 1947)
All My Sons (Univ., 1948)
Key Largo (WB, 1948)
The Night Has a Thousand Eyes (Par., 1948)
House of Strangers (20th, 1949)
It's a Great Feeling (WB, 1949)

My Daughter Joy (Col., 1950)
Actors and Sin (UA, 1952)
Vice Squad (UA, 1953)
The Big Leaguer (MGM, 1953)
The Glass Web (Univ., 1953)
Black Tuesday (UA, 1954)
The Violent Men (Col., 1955)
Tight Spot (Col., 1955)
A Bullet for Joey (UA, 1955)
Illegal (WB, 1955)
Hell on Frisco Bay (WB, 1955)
Nightmare (UA, 1956)
The Ten Commandments (Par., 1956)
A Hole in the Head (UA, 1959)
Seven Thieves (20th, 1960)
Pepe (Col., 1960)
My Geisha (Par., 1962)
Two Weeks in Another Town (MGM, 1962)
Sammy Going South (Bryanston, 1963)
The Prize (MGM, 1963)
Good Neighbor Sam (Col., 1964)
Robin and the Seven Hoods (WB, 1964)
Cheyenne Autumn (WB, 1964)
The Outrage (MGM, 1964)
The Cincinnati Kid (MGM, 1965)
The Biggest Bundle of Them All (MGM, 1968)
Grand Slam (Par., 1968)
MacKenna's Gold (Col., 1968)
Operation St. Peter's (Ultra-Marianne, 1968)
Soylent Green (MGM, 1973)

Will Rogers
(1879–1935)

Will Rogers was born in Oolagah Indian Territory, which is now Oklahoma, of Irish and Indian ancestors. Educated in a military academy, he learned to ride and do lariat tricks and then worked as a ranch hand and cow-puncher. After a job on a ship which supplied mules for the British in the Boer War, he joined a wild west show in Johannesburg and was billed as *The Cherokee Kid*. He returned to the States, toured at fairs and appeared at the St. Louis World's Fair of 1904 and the Madison Square Garden Annual Horse Fair.

Rogers next toured in vaudeville doing rope tricks. He added dialog to his act, commenting on public figures and current happenings. This led to musical comedy and Ziegfeld's *Midnight Frolic* supper show. After starring in The Ziegfeld Follies of 1917 and 1918 he was put under contract by Samuel Goldwyn and made several films for him and one for Paramount. He then decided to produce, direct, write and act in his own two-reelers.

Top: It's *State Fair* time and Louise Dresser is busy fixing her pickles for the cooking contest. Will Rogers plays her husband (Fox, 1933). *Bottom:* The story of two opposing clans from the hills starred Will Rogers in his last film *In Old Kentucky* with Bill Robinson *(left)* and Dorothy Wilson (Fox, 1935).

Will Rogers is the steamboat captain who races against time to save an innocent man from being hanged in *Steamboat 'Round the Bend* **(Fox, 1935).**

Will Rogers worked briefly for Hal Roach before going on a successful tour. He began to write for newspapers and magazines and then returned to Broadway in a musical. With the arrival of the "talkies" Fox signed him to a long-term contract and he became a box office champion. He was deeply interested in aviation and was a good friend of Wiley Post, the famous aviator. In 1935 they were both killed in a plane crash in Alaska.

Will Rogers Sound Feature Films (1929–1935)

They Had to See Paris (Fox, 1929)

Happy Days (Fox, 1930)

So This Is London (Fox, 1930)

Lightnin' (Fox, 1930)

A Connecticut Yankee (Fox, 1931)

Young As You Feel (Fox, 1931)

Ambassador Bill (Fox, 1931)

Business and Pleasure (Fox, 1932)

Down to Earth (Fox, 1932)

Too Busy to Work (Fox, 1932)

State Fair (Fox, 1933)

Doctor Bull (Fox, 1933)
Mr. Skitch (Fox, 1933)
David Harum (Fox, 1934)
Handy Andy (Fox, 1934)
Judge Priest (Fox, 1934)
County Chairman (Fox, 1935)

Life Begins at 40 (Fox, 1935)
Doubting Thomas (Fox, 1935)
In Old Kentucky (Fox, 1935)
Steamboat 'Round the Bend (Fox, 1935)

Rosalind Russell
(1907–1976)

Rosalind Russell was born in Waterbury, Connecticut, the daughter of a lawyer and a fashion editor. She appeared in *Garrick Gaities* in 1926 and then spent three years in stock. Her role in the play *Talent* (1932) led to parts in Theatre Guild offerings. During her appearance in *The Second Man* Universal paid her way to Hollywood for a test. While waiting for a Universal contract, she did the play *No More Ladies* in Los Angeles. MGM tested her and she signed a contract with that studio. She played small parts in various films until she appeared opposite Paul Lukas in *The Casino Murder Case.* When Myrna Loy refused to do *Rendezvous* Rosalind Russell replaced her. She appeared opposite top leading men on her home lot and on loan to various studios. In *The Women* she stole the film from the other female stars. On loan she made the classic *His Girl Friday* opposite Cary Grant. Her following films through 1952 were disappointing. She toured in *Bell, Book and Candle* with Dennis Price and then did the Broadway musical *Wonderful Town* which made her the toast of Broadway. Returning to films, she again appeared in a series of disappointing roles. She starred again on Broadway in the smash hit *Auntie Mame* and repeated the role with great success in a film. In 1972 she received a special Oscar, the Jean Hersholt Humanitarian Award for her charity work. She died in 1976 of cancer. A memoir, *Life Is a Banquet*, was published after her death.

Rosalind Russell Feature Films (1934–1971)

Evelyn Prentice (MGM, 1934)
The President Vanishes (Par., 1934)

West Point of the Air (MGM, 1935)

Rosalind Russell, an aggressive stage mother with two daughters to support, meets agent Karl Malden and they fall in love in *Gypsy* (Warner Bros., 1962).

Casino Murder Case (MGM, 1935)
Reckless (MGM, 1935)
China Seas (MGM, 1935)
Rendezvous (MGM, 1935)
Forsaking All Others (MGM, 1935)
The Night Is Young (MGM, 1935)

It Had to Happen (20th, 1936)
Under Two Flags (20th, 1936)
Trouble for Two (MGM, 1936)
Craig's Wife (Col., 1936)
Night Must Fall (MGM, 1937)
Live, Love and Learn (MGM, 1937)
Man-Proof (MGM, 1938)
The Citadel (MGM, 1938)

Rosalind Russell and Clark Gable are jewel thieves in the adventure comedy *They Met in Bombay* (MGM, 1941).

Four's a Crowd (WB, 1938)
Fast and Loose (MGM, 1939)
The Women (MGM, 1939)
His Girl Friday (Col., 1940)
No Time for Comedy (WB, 1940)
Hired Wife (Univ., 1940)
Thing Thing Called Love (Col., 1941)
They Met in Bombay (MGM, 1941)
The Feminine Touch (MGM, 1941)
Design for Scandal (MGM, 1941)
Take a Letter, Darling (Par., 1942)
My Sister Eileen (Col., 1942)
Flight for Freedom (RKO, 1943)
What a Woman (Col., 1943)
Roughly Speaking (WB, 1945)
She Wouldn't Say Yes (Col., 1945)
Sister Kenny (RKO, 1946)
The Guilt of Janet Ames (Col., 1947)
Mourning Becomes Electra (RKO, 1947)
The Velvet Touch (RKO, 1948)
Tell It to the Judge (Col., 1949)
A Woman of Distinction (Col., 1950)
Never Wave at a WAC (RKO, 1952)
The Girl Rush (Par., 1955)
Picnic (Col., 1955)
Auntie Mame (WB, 1958)
A Majority of One (WB, 1961)
Five Finger Exercise (Col., 1962)
Gypsy (WB, 1962)
The Trouble with Angels (Col., 1966)

*Oh Dad, Poor Dad, Mama's
Hung You in the Closet and
I'm Feeling So Sad* (Par., 1967)
Where Angels Go... Trouble

Follows (Col., 1968)
Rosie! (Univ., 1968)
Unexpected Mrs. Pollifax (UA,
1971)

Randolph Scott
(1898–1987)

Randolph Scott was born in Orange, Virginia, educated in private schools and attended Georgia Tech where he played football. After a football injury he transferred to the University of North Carolina and studied engineering but decided on an acting career. His father gave him a letter of introduction to Howard Hughes who got him a bit part in a silent film. More extra work followed. Scott decided he needed theatre training and enrolled at the Pasadena Community Theatre where he studied for two years. While appearing there in *Under a Virginia Moon* he did a screen test for Paramount. They signed him to a seven-year contract which led to screen stardom. He appeared opposite Margaret Sullavan, Irene Dunne, Ginger Rogers, Joan Bennett, Marlene Dietrich, and Mae West. Until his retirement he dominated the Western movies and was listed among the top box office stars. He became a multimillionaire through real estate investments. He was married briefly to heiress Maraianna du Pont in 1936. In 1944 he married Marie Stillman. They had a daughter, Sandra, and a son, Christopher. After being in ill health for several years he died of natural causes.

Randolph Scott Feature Films (1931–1962)

The Women Men Marry (Headline Pictures, 1931)
Sky Bride (Par., 1932)
Hot Saturday (Par., 1932)
Wild Horse Mesa (Par., 1933)
Hello, Everybody! (Par., 1933)
Murders in the Zoo (Par., 1933)

Heritage of the Desert (Par., 1933)
Supernatural (Par., 1933)
Sunset Pass (Par., 1933)
Cocktail Hour (Col., 1933)
Man of the Forest (Par., 1933)
To the Last Man (Par., 1933)

A former Confederate soldier (Randolph Scott) tries to start a new life in Arizona. Adele Jergins *(seated)* and Hope Landin are interested parties in *Sugarfoot* (Warner Bros., 1951).

Broken Dreams (Mon., 1933)
The Thundering Herd (Par., 1933)
Last Round-Up (Par., 1934)
The Lone Cowboy (Par., 1934)
Wagon Wheels (Par., 1934)
Rocky Mountain Mystery (Par., 1935)
Roberta (Par., 1935)
Home on the Range (Par., 1935)

Village Tale (RKO, 1935)
She (RKO, 1935)
So Red the Rose (Par., 1935)
Follow the Fleet (RKO, 1936)
And Sudden Death (Par., 1936)
The Last of the Mohicans (UA, 1936)
Go West Young Man (Par., 1936)

Randolph Scott *(seated)* questions an Indian about a wagon full of gold that has been buried for years in Death Valley in *The Walking Hills* (Columbia, 1949).

High, Wide and Handsome (Par., 1937)
Rebecca of Sunnybrook Farm (20th, 1938)
Road to Reno (Univ., 1938)
The Texans (Par., 1938)
Jesse James (20th, 1939)
Susannah of the Mounties (20th, 1939)
Coast Guard (Col., 1939)
Frontier Marshal (20th, 1939)
20,000 Men a Year (20th, 1939)
Virginia City (WB, 1940)

My Favorite Wife (RKO, 1940)
When the Daltons Rode (Univ., 1940)
Western Union (20th, 1941)
Belle Starr (20th, 1941)
Paris Calling (Univ., 1941)
To the Shores of Tripoli (20th, 1942)
The Spoilers (Univ., 1942)
Pittsburgh (Univ., 1942)
The Desperadoes (Col., 1943)
Bombadier (RKO, 1943)
Corvette K-225 (Univ., 1943)

Gung Ho! (Univ., 1943)
Belle of the Yukon (RKO, 1944)
Follow the Boys (Univ., 1944)
China Sky (RKO, 1945)
Captain Kidd (UA, 1945)
Abilene Town (UA, 1946)
Badman's Territory (RKO, 1946)
Home Sweet Homicide (20th, 1946)
Trail Street (RKO, 1947)
Gunfighters (Col., 1947)
Christmas Eve (UA, 1947)
Albuquerque (Par., 1948)
Return of the Bad Men (RKO, 1948)
Coroner Creek (Col., 1948)
Canadian Pacific (20th, 1949)
The Walking Hills (Col., 1949)
The Doolins of Oklahoma (Col., 1949)
Fighting Man of the Plains (20th, 1949)
The Nevadan (Col., 1950)
Colt .45 (WB, 1950)
The Cariboo Trail (20th, 1950)
Sugarfoot (WB, 1951)
Starlift (WB, 1951)
Santa Fe (Col., 1951)
Fort Worth (WB, 1951)
Man in the Saddle (Col., 1951)

Carson City (WB, 1952)
Hangman's Knot (Col., 1952)
The Man Behind the Gun (WB, 1952)
The Stranger Wore a Gun (Col., 1953)
Thunder Over the Plains (WB, 1953)
Riding Shotgun (WB, 1954)
The Bounty Hunter (WB, 1954)
Rage at Dawn (RKO, 1955)
Ten Wanted Men (Col., 1955)
Tall Man Riding (WB, 1955)
A Lawless Street (Col., 1955)
Seven Men From Now (WB, 1956)
Seventh Cavalry (Col., 1956)
The Tall T (Col., 1957)
Shoot-Out at Medicine Bend (WB, 1957)
Decision At Sundown (Col., 1957)
Buchanan Rides Alone (Col., 1958)
Ride Lonesome (Col., 1959)
Westbound (WB, 1959)
Comanche Station (Col., 1960)
Ride the High Country (MGM, 1962)

Norma Shearer
(1900–1983)

Norma Shearer was born in the Montreal suburb of Westmount. She left school at 14 to begin a stage career with her sister Athole under the guidance of their mother. In New York both sisters got minor roles on the stage and in films. Athole married Howard Hawks and abandoned her acting ambitions while Norma went into modeling and became "Miss Lotta Miles" for Kelly-Springfield Tire advertisements.

Leslie Howard and Norma Shearer as *Romeo and Juliet* fall in love despite their families' enmitys in the classic Shakespeare tragedy (MGM, 1936).

Receiving a contract with Louis B. Mayer, she went to Hollywood and was cast in many successful films at MGM and on loan to other studios. She married Irving Thalberg in 1927, had two children, Irving, Jr. and Katherine, and was widowed in 1936. She won an Academy Award in 1929 for her performance in *The Divorcee* and was nominated five other times.

In 1942 she married ski instructor Martin Arrouge and retired from films. Over the years she was offered many roles but turned them down. She did not appear in public or receive visitors after September, 1980, when she was in failing health and moved to The Motion Picture and Television Country House in Woodland, California. She died there in 1983.

Norma Shearer as Mary Haines tells her mother (Lucile Watson) she has learned that her husband is unfaithful in *The Women* (MGM, 1939).

Norma Shearer Sound Feature Films (1929–1942)

The Trial of Mary Dugan (MGM, 1929)
The Last of Mrs. Cheyney (MGM, 1929)
The Hollywood Revue (MGM, 1929)
Their Own Desire (MGM, 1930)
The Divorcee (MGM, 1930)
Let Us Be Gay (MGM, 1930)
Strangers May Kiss (MGM, 1931)
A Free Soul (MGM, 1931)
Private Lives (MGM, 1931)
Strange Interlude (MGM, 1932)
Smilin' Through (MGM, 1932)
Riptide (MGM, 1934)
The Barretts of Wimploe Street (MGM, 1934)
Romeo and Juliet (MGM, 1936)
Marie Antoinette (MGM, 1938)
Idiot's Delight (MGM, 1939)
The Women (MGM, 1939)
Escape (MGM, 1940)
We Were Dancing (MGM, 1942)
Her Cardboard Lover (MGM, 1942)

Ann Sheridan
(1915–1967)

Ann Sheridan was born in Denton, Texas, and while a student at North Texas State Teachers' College she was a winner in Paramount's

Search for Beauty contest in 1933. She was signed to a starlet's contract and appeared in bit roles under her real name, Clara Lou Sheridan. In 1935 she was billed as Ann Sheridan. A year later she signed with Warner Brothers where she remained under contract until 1948. At that studio she was billed as the ·*Oomph Girl* and appeared in many melodramas. In *King's Row* (1942) she proved she had great acting ability. She showed her versatility by appearing in comedies and musicals. Her leading men included James Cagney, Errol Flynn, George Raft, Ronald Reagan, Dick Powell, Gary Cooper and Cary Grant. She appeared in stock and in the NBC daytime soap opera *Another World*. At the time of her death she was starring in the successful television series *Pistols and Petticoats*. She had been married to Edward Norris, George Brent and Scott McKay.

Ann Sheridan Feature Films (1934–1957)

As Clara Lou Sheridan:
Search for Beauty (Par., 1934)
Bolero (Par., 1934)
Come On, Marines (Par., 1934)
Murder at the Vanities (Par., 1934)
Kiss and Make Up (Par., 1934)
Shoot the Works (Par., 1934)
Notorious Sophie Lang (Par., 1934)
Ladies Should Listen (Par., 1934)
Wagon Wheels (Par., 1934)
Mrs. Wiggs of the Cabbage Patch (Par., 1934)
College Rhythm (Par., 1934)
You Belong to Me (Par., 1934)
Limehouse Blues (Par., 1934)
Enter Madame (Par., 1935)
Home on the Range (Par., 1935)
Rumba (Par., 1935)

As Ann Sheridan:
Behold My Wife (Par., 1935)
Car 99 (Par., 1935)
Rocky Mountain Mystery (Par., 1935)
Mississippi (Par., 1935)
The Glass Key (Par., 1935)
The Crusades (Par., 1935)
Red Blood of Courage (Ambassador, 1935)
Fighting Youth (Univ., 1935)
Sing Me a Love Song (WB, 1936)
Black Legion (WB, 1936)
The Great O'Malley (WB, 1937)
San Quentin (WB, 1937)
Wine, Women and Horses (WB, 1937)
The Footloose Heiress (WB, 1937)
Alcatraz Island (WB, 1938)
She Loved a Fireman (WB, 1938)
The Patient in Room 18 (WB, 1938)
Mystery House (WB, 1938)

Cary Grant as a French officer and Ann Sheridan as a WAC lieutenant play a married couple dealing with government regulations and red tape in *I Was a Male War Bride* (20th Century–Fox, 1949).

Cowboy from Brooklyn (WB, 1938)

Little Miss Thoroughbred (WB, 1938)

Letter of Introduction (Univ., 1938)

Broadway Musketeers (WB, 1938)

Angels with Dirty Faces (WB, 1938)

They Made Me a Criminal (WB, 1939)

Dodge City (WB, 1939)

Naughty but Nice (WB, 1939)

Winter Carnival (UA, 1939)

Indianapolis Speedway (WB, 1939)

Angels Wash Their Faces (WB, 1939)

Castle on the Hudson (WB, 1940)

It All Came True (WB, 1940)

Torrid Zone (WB, 1940)

They Drive By Night (WB, 1940)

City for Conquest (WB, 1940)

Honeymoon for Three (WB, 1941)

Navy Blues (WB, 1941)

The Man Who Came to Dinner (WB, 1941)

Juke Girl (WB, 1942)

Wings for the Eagle (WB, 1942)

George Washington Slept Here (WB, 1942)

Edge of Darkness (WB, 1943)

Ann Sheridan is a saloon singer on the run from the law who hides out in a Northwest lumber camp. Sterling Hayden is a logger and part-time minister in *Take Me to Town* (Universal, 1953).

Thank Your Lucky Stars (WB, 1943)
Shine On, Harvest Moon (WB, 1944)
The Doughgirls (WB, 1944)
One More Tomorrow (WB, 1946)
Nora Prentiss (WB, 1947)
The Unfaithful (WB, 1947)
Treasure of the Sierra Madre (unbilled guest appearance; WB, 1948)
Silver River (WB, 1948)
Good Sam (RKO, 1948)
I Was a Male War Bride (20th, 1949)
Stella (20th, 1950)
Woman on the Run (Univ., 1950)
Steel Town (Univ., 1952)
Just Across the Street (Univ., 1952)
Take Me to Town (Univ., 1953)
Appointment in Honduras (RKO, 1953)
Come Next Spring (Rep., 1956)
The Opposite Sex (MGM, 1956)
Woman and the Hunter (Gross-Krasne-Phoenix, 1957)

Margaret Sullavan
(1911–1960)

James Stewart *(center)* is a World War I soldier who meets Margaret Sullavan and falls in love. Walter Pidgeon is the other man in *The Shopworn Angel* (MGM, 1938).

Margaret Sullavan was born in Norfolk, Virginia, of a well-to-do family. She first acted with the Baltimore University Players and then studied dancing and acting in Boston. At 17 she made her professional stage debut with the famed University Players of Cape Cod. Henry Fonda and James Stewart were in the company. She was married briefly to Fonda and continued her acting career touring in plays. She then signed a contract with the Shuberts. When she took over the ingenue role in *Dinner at Eight* director John M. Stahl saw her. She was tested for the leading role in *Only Yesterday,* which she won. She married director William Wyler and divorced him while under contract to Universal. Sullavan next married agent Leland Hayward and he arranged a contract for her at Metro-Goldwyn-Mayer. She won the New York Film Critics Award for her performance in *Three Comrades.* Returning to Broadway in *Voice of the Turtle,* she won the Drama Critics Award

Margaret Sullavan comes to *The Little Shop Around the Corner.* James Stewart *(center)* is the top clerk and Frank Morgan is the owner of the shop (MGM, 1940).

and also did the play in London. Her marriage to Hayward ended in divorce. She made her last film, *No Sad Songs for Me,* at Columbia and appeared on Broadway in such hit plays as *The Deep Blue Sea, Sabrina Fair* and *Janus.* She died of an overdose of barbituates while in a tryout for a new play in 1960.

Margaret Sullavan Feature Films (1933–1950)

Only Yesterday (Univ., 1933)
Little Man, What Now? (Univ., 1934)
The Good Fairy (Univ., 1935)
So Red the Rose (Par., 1935)

Next Time We Love (Univ., 1936)
The Moon's Our Home (Par., 1936)
Three Comrades (MGM, 1938)

The Shopworn Angel (MGM, 1938)
The Shining Hour (MGM, 1938)
The Shop Around the Corner (MGM, 1940)
The Mortal Storm (MGM, 1940)
So Ends Our Night (UA, 1941)

Back Street (Univ., 1941)
Appointment for Love (Univ., 1941)
Cry Havoc (MGM, 1943)
No Sad Songs for Me (Col., 1950)

Gloria Swanson
(1898–1983)

Teacher-lover Ferdinand Gottschalk tells opera singer Gloria Swanson that she lacks the requisite fire and passion to be a diva in *Tonight or Never* (United Artists, 1931).

Gloria Swanson was born in Chicago. Her father was a civilian employee of the government and as a child she lived on many Army

Opposite: Robert Taylor, Franchot Tone and Robert Young are three returning German soldiers and Margaret Sullavan is an impoverished beauty with incurable tuberculosis in *Three Comrades* (MGM, 1938).

As Norma Desmond, Gloria Swanson plays an aging silent film star who lives in a dream world that becomes a nightmare in *Sunset Boulevard* (Par., 1950).

bases in the United States and the Philippines. Returning to Chicago, she worked as a notions clerk and studied singing. She did extra work and bit parts at Essanay. She met Wallace Beery there and married him in 1916. This union lasted until after they went to Hollywood in 1919. Mack Sennett hired her and she made films for him before moving briefly to Triangle Studios. She then signed with Paramount and became a top star under the direction of Cecil B. DeMille. Wanting more control of her films, she became an independent producer with the help of Joseph P. Kennedy. While making a film in France she married the Marquis de la Falaise de la Coudraye but the marriage failed. She then married Michael Farmer. She made a successful transition from silent films to the talkies and was nominated three times for the Oscar. Dissatisfied with Hollywood, she turned to the stage and toured in *Reflected Glory.* Between stage work she returned occasionally in Hollywood roles. In 1950 she was a sensational success in the movie *Sunset Boulevard* for Wilder-Brackett. On Broadway she starred opposite Jose Ferrer in the revival of *Twentieth Century,* David Niven in *Nina* and in *Butterflies Are Free.* She appeared on television and wrote her autobiography *Swanson on Swanson* which was published in 1980. After a brief illness she died in New York at the age of 84.

Gloria Swanson Sound Film Credits (1930–1975)

What a Widow! (UA, 1930)
Indiscreet (UA, 1931)
Tonight or Never (UA, 1931)
Perfect Understanding (UA, 1933)
Music in the Air (Fox, 1934)

Father Takes a Wife (RKO, 1941)
Sunset Boulevard (Par., 1950)
Three for Bedroom C (WB, 1952)
Airport (Univ., 1975)

Robert Taylor
(1911–1969)

Robert Taylor was born in Filley, Nebraska, the son of a country doctor. He attended Doane College where he was a music major. He then went to Pomona College in California and enrolled in the drama department. While in a college stage production of *Journey's End* he was screen tested and signed a contract with MGM in 1934. He remained with the studio until 1958. He was loaned to Fox and Universal before scoring a hit in MGM's short *Buried Loot* of their *Crime Does Not Pay* series. With careful grooming by the studio he became a box office winner. He was loaned to Universal opposite Irene Dunne in *The Magnificent Obsession,* causing him to be in demand as a leading man. He appeared opposite Janet Gaynor, Loretta Young, Joan Crawford, Greta Garbo, and Barbara Stanwyck, whom he married in 1939. The union lasted until 1952. During World War II he served as a flight instructor

Robert Taylor plays a Broadway producer and Eleanor Powell is his old flame who comes to New York hoping he will cast her in *Broadway Melody of 1936* (MGM, 1935).

for two years. He also directed many training films and was the narrator of the feature documentary *The Fighting Lady*. After the service he returned to films at MGM. In 1954 he married Ursula Thiess. She was widowed in 1969 when Taylor died of lung cancer.

Robert Taylor Feature Films (1934–1968)

Handy Andy (Fox, 1934)
There's Always Tomorrow (Univ., 1934)
Wicked Woman (MGM, 1934)
Society Doctor (MGM, 1935)
West Point of the Air (MGM, 1935)
Times Square Lady (MGM, 1935)
Murder in the Fleet (MGM, 1935)
Broadway Melody of 1936 (MGM, 1935)

As an undercover investigator Robert Taylor joins Victor McLaglen and his gang of bank robbers in *This Is My Affair* (20th Century–Fox, 1937).

Magnificent Obsession (Univ., 1935)
Small Town Girl (MGM, 1936)
Private Number (20th, 1936)
His Brother's Wife (MGM, 1936)
The Gorgeous Hussy (MGM, 1936)
Camille (MGM, 1936)
Personal Property (MGM, 1937)
This Is My Affair (20th, 1937)
Broadway Melody of 1938 (MGM, 1937)
A Yank at Oxford (MGM, 1938)

Three Comrades (MGM, 1938)
The Crowd Roars (MGM, 1938)
Stand Up and Fight (MGM, 1939)
Lady Luck (MGM, 1939)
Lady of the Tropics (MGM, 1939)
Remember? (MGM, 1939)
Waterloo Bridge (MGM, 1940)
Escape (MGM, 1940)
Flight Command (MGM, 1940)
Billy the Kid (MGM, 1941)
When Ladies Meet (MGM, 1941)

Johnny Eager (MGM, 1942)
Her Cardboard Lover (MGM, 1942)
Stand By for Action (MGM, 1943)
The Youngest Profession (unbilled guest appearance; MGM, 1943)
Bataan (MGM, 1943)
Song of Russia (MGM, 1944)
Undercurrent (MGM, 1946)
The High Wall (MGM, 1947)
The Secret Land (narrator; MGM, 1948)
The Bribe (MGM, 1949)
Ambush (MGM, 1949)
Devil's Doorway (MGM, 1950)
Conspirator (MGM, 1950)
Quo Vadis (MGM, 1951)
Westward the Women (MGM, 1951)
Ivanhoe (MGM, 1952)
Above and Beyond (MGM, 1952)
I Love Melvin (unbilled guest appearance; MGM, 1953)
Ride, Vaquero! (MGM, 1953)
All the Brothers Were Valiant (MGM, 1953)
Knights of the Round Table (MGM, 1953)
Valley of the Kings (MGM, 1954)
Rogue Cop (MGM, 1954)
Many Rivers to Cross (MGM, 1955)
Quentin Durward (MGM, 1955)
The Last Hunt (MGM, 1956)
D-Day, the Sixth of June (20th, 1956)
The Power and the Prize (MGM, 1956)
Tip on a Dead Jockey (MGM, 1957)
Saddle the Wind (MGM, 1958)
The Law and Jake Wade (MGM, 1958)
Party Girl (MGM, 1958)
The Hangman (Par., 1959)
The House of the Seven Hawks (MGM, 1959)
Killers of Kilimanjaro (Col., 1960)
The Miracle of the White Stallions (BV, 1963)
Cattle King (MGM, 1963)
A House Is Not a Home (Embassy, 1964)
The Night Walker (Univ., 1965)
Savage Pampas (Daca, 1966)
Johnny Tiger (Univ., 1966)
Where Angels Go...Trouble Follows (Col., 1968)
The Day the Hot Line Got Hot (AIP, 1968)
Devil May Care (Feature Film Corp. of America, 1968)
The Glass Sphinx (AIP, 1968)

Spencer Tracy
(1900–1967)

Spencer Tracy was born in Milwaukee, Wisconsin, the son of a truck salesman. In 1917 he interrupted his Jesuit prep school education and joined the navy. After World War I he entered Ripon College

Top: Spencer Tracy marries schoolteacher Colleen Moore and with her guidance through hard work and sacrifice becomes the president of a railroad company in *The Power and the Glory* (Fox, 1933). *Bottom:* Spencer Tracy and Katharine Hepburn co-starred in their last film together, *Guess Who's Coming to Dinner.* It is the story of the marriage of their daughter to a black research physician (Columbia, 1967).

Jean Simmons, *right*, (as the daughter of Teresa Wright and Spencer Tracy) wants to pursue a stage career in *The Actress* (MGM, 1953).

(Wisconsin) and appeared in a college stage production. In 1922 he enrolled at the American Academy of Dramatic Arts in New York and that same year made his Broadway debut in a bit role in the classic play *R.U.R.* He toured in stock and in 1923 married stage actress Louise Treadwell. On Broadway he appeared with Ethel Barrymore and George M. Cohan before scoring a hit in *The Last Mile.* He made two shorts for Vitaphone and was tested by various studios. They all considered him unsuitable for films. Director John Ford saw him on stage and requested Fox to sign him to a contract. He got the lead in Ford's film *Up the River.* From 1930 to 1935 he had a stormy relationship with Fox but a much better one with Warner Brothers and MGM while on loan to them. Irving Thalberg of MGM persuaded his studio to sign Tracy. Under MGM's banner he became a box office favorite. He won best actor Academy Awards for *Captains Courageous* in 1937 and *Boys Town* in 1938. In the following years (to 1967) he was nominated seven more times. In 1942 Tracy and Katharine Hepburn first co-starred in

Woman of the Year. From then to 1967 they appeared as a team in nine successful films. He returned to the stage with glowing reviews in the ill-fated Robert Sherwood play *The Rugged Path.* After his MGM contract ended he free-lanced, carefully selecting his films.

Spencer Tracy Feature Films (1930–1967)

Up the River (Fox, 1930)
Quick Millions (Fox, 1931)
Six Cylinder Love (Fox, 1931)
Goldie (Fox, 1931)
She Wanted a Millionaire (Fox, 1932)
Sky Devils (UA, 1932)
Disorderly Conduct (Fox, 1932)
Young America (Fox, 1932)
Society Girl (Fox, 1932)
Painted Woman (Fox, 1932)
Me and My Gal (Fox, 1932)
20,000 Years in Sing Sing (WB, 1933)
Face in the Sky (Fox, 1933)
The Power and the Glory (Fox, 1933)
Shanghai Madness (Fox, 1933)
The Mad Game (Fox, 1933)
Man's Castle (Col., 1933)
Looking for Trouble (UA, 1934)
The Show-Off (MGM, 1934)
Bottoms Up (Fox, 1934)
Now I'll Tell (Fox, 1934)
Marie Galante (Fox, 1934)
It's a Small World (Fox, 1935)
Murder Man (MGM, 1935)
Dante's Inferno (Fox, 1935)
Whipsaw (MGM, 1935)
Riffraff (MGM, 1936)
Fury (MGM, 1936)
San Francisco (MGM, 1936)
Libeled Lady (MGM, 1936)
Captains Courageous (MGM, 1937)
They Gave Him a Gun (MGM, 1937)
The Big City (MGM, 1937)
Mannequin (MGM, 1938)
Test Pilot (MGM, 1938)
Boys Town (MGM, 1938)
Stanley and Livingstone (20th, 1939)
I Take This Woman (MGM, 1940)
Northwest Passage (MGM, 1940)
Edison the Man (MGM, 1940)
Boom Town (MGM, 1940)
Men of Boys Town (MGM, 1941)
Dr. Jekyll and Mr. Hyde (MGM, 1941)
Woman of the Year (MGM, 1942)
Tortilla Flat (MGM, 1942)
Keeper of the Flame (MGM, 1942)
A Guy Named Joe (MGM, 1943)
The Seventh Cross (MGM, 1944)
Thirty Seconds Over Tokyo (MGM, 1944)
Without Love (MGM, 1945)
The Sea of Grass (MGM, 1947)
Cass Timberlane (MGM, 1947)
State of the Union (MGM, 1948)
Edward, My Son (MGM, 1949)
Adam's Rib (MGM, 1949)
Malaya (MGM, 1949)
Father of the Bride (MGM, 1950)
Father's Little Dividend (MGM, 1951)

The People Against O'Hara
(MGM, 1951)
Pat and Mike (MGM, 1952)
Plymouth Adventure (MGM,
1952)
The Actress (MGM, 1953)
Broken Lance (20th, 1954)
Bad Day at Black Rock (MGM,
1955)
The Mountain (Par., 1956)
The Desk Set (20th, 1957)
The Old Man and the Sea (WB,
1958)

The Last Hurrah (Col., 1958)
Inherit the Wind (UA, 1960)
The Devil at 4 O'Clock (Col.,
1961)
Judgment at Nuremberg (UA,
1961)
How the West Was Won (MGM,
1963)
*It's a Mad, Mad, Mad, Mad
World* (UA, 1963)
Guess Who's Coming to Dinner
(Col., 1967)

John Wayne
(1907–1979)

John Wayne

John Wayne (born Marion Morrison) was the son of a druggist in Winterset, Iowa. He attended the University of Southern California on a football scholarship and during vacations he worked at Fox studios as a laborer and prop man. He met director John Ford who cast him in bit roles which led to the lead in Raoul Walsh's film *The Big Trail.* Following a brief contract with Fox he signed with Columbia where he was a featured player and star of Westerns. He next appeared in two serials and in pictures for Warner Brothers. From 1933 to 1935 Wayne made Westerns for Monogram.

Randolph Scott *(left)* **and John Wayne are rugged coal miners who fall in love with Marlene Dietrich in** *Pittsburgh* **(Universal, 1942).**

After a brief contract with Universal he signed with Republic Studio. In 1939 John Ford made the classic *Stagecoach* and cast him in the lead. Following the success of that film other studios borrowed him from Republic and his home studio began producing big budget films with him in the lead. With John Ford as his director, he became a box office champion for 23 years. In 1969 he won an Academy Award for the film *True Grit.* He set up his own producing company, Batjac, and produced, directed and starred in various films before his death of cancer in 1979.

John Wayne Sound Feature Films (1929–1976)

Salute (Fox, 1929)
Men Without Women (Fox, 1930)
Rough Romance (Fox, 1930)

Girls Demand Excitement (Fox, 1931)
Three Girls Lost (Fox, 1931)
Men Are Like That (Col., 1931)

Range Feud (Col., 1931)
Hurricane Express (Mascot serial, 1932)
Shadow of the Eagle (Mascot serial, 1932)
Maker of Men (Col., 1932)
Two Fisted Law (Col., 1932)
Texas Cyclone (Col., 1932)
Lady and Gent (Par., 1932)
Ride Him Cowboy (WB, 1932)
The Big Stampede (WB, 1932)
The Three Musketeers (Mascot serial, 1933)
Haunted Gold (WB, 1933)
Telegraph Trail (WB, 1933)
His Private Secretary (Showman's Pictures, 1933)
Central Airport (WB, 1933)
Somewhere in Sonora (WB, 1933)
The Life of Jimmy Dolan (WB, 1933)
Baby Face (WB, 1933)
The Man from Monterey (WB, 1933)
Riders of Destiny (Mon., 1933)
College Coach (WB, 1933)
West of the Divide (Mon., 1934)
Blue Steel (Mon., 1934)
Lucky Texan (Mon., 1934)
The Man from Utah (Mon., 1934)
Randy Rides Alone (Mon., 1934)
The Star Packer (Mon., 1934)
The Trail Beyond (Mon., 1934)
'Neath Arizona Skies (Mon., 1934)
Texas Terror (Mon., 1935)
The Lawless Frontier (Mon., 1935)
Rainbow Valley (Mon., 1935)

Paradise Canyon (Mon., 1935)
The Dawn Rider (Mon., 1935)
Westward Ho! (Rep., 1935)
Desert Trail (Mon., 1935)
The Lawless 90's (Rep., 1936)
King of the Pecos (Rep., 1936)
The Oregon Trail (Rep., 1936)
Winds of the Wasteland (Rep., 1936)
The Sea Spoilers (Univ., 1936)
The Lonely Trail (Rep., 1936)
Conflict (Univ., 1936)
California Straight Ahead (Univ., 1937)
I Cover the War (Univ., 1937)
Idol of the Crowds (Univ., 1937)
Adventure's End (Univ., 1937)
Born to the West (Par., 1938)
Pals of the Saddle (Rep., 1938)
Overland Stage Raiders (Rep., 1938)
Santa Fe Stampede (Rep., 1938)
Red River Range (Rep., 1938)
Stagecoach (UA, 1939)
Night Riders (Rep., 1939)
Three Texas Steers (Rep., 1939)
Wyoming Outlaw (Rep., 1939)
New Frontier (Rep., 1939)
Allegheny Uprising (RKO, 1939)
Dark Command (Rep., 1940)
Three Faces West (Rep., 1940)
The Long Voyage Home (UA, 1940)
Seven Sinners (Univ., 1940)
A Man Betrayed (Rep., 1941)
The Lady from Louisiana (Rep., 1941)
The Shepherd of the Hills (Par., 1941)
Lady for a Night (Rep., 1941)
Reap the Wild Wind (Par., 1942)

Opposite, from left: Claire Trevor, John Wayne, Andy Devine, John Carradine, Louise Platt, Thomas Mitchell, Berton Churchill, Donald Meek and George Bancroft in *Stagecoach*. This classic western directed by John Ford tells of frontier life in the untamed great Southwest (United Artists, 1939).

The Spoilers (Univ., 1942)
In Old California (Rep., 1942)
The Flying Tigers (Rep., 1942)
Reunion (MGM, 1942)
Pittsburgh (Univ., 1942)
A Lady Takes a Chance (RKO, 1943)
In Old Oklahoma (Rep., 1943)
The Fighting Seabees (Rep., 1944)
Tall in the Saddle (RKO, 1944)
Back to Bataan (RKO, 1945)
Flame of the Barbary Coast (Rep., 1945)
Dakota (Rep., 1945)
They Were Expendable (MGM, 1945)
Without Reservations (RKO, 1946)
Angel and the Badman (Rep., 1947)
Tycoon (RKO, 1947)
Fort Apache (RKO, 1948)
Red River (UA, 1948)
Three Godfathers (MGM, 1948)
Wake of the Red Witch (Rep., 1948)
The Fighting Kentuckian (Rep., 1949)
She Wore a Yellow Ribbon (RKO, 1949)
Sands of Iwo Jima (Rep., 1949)
Rio Grande (Rep., 1950)
Operation Pacific (WB, 1951)
Flying Leathernecks (RKO, 1951)
Big Jim McLain (WB, 1952)
The Quiet Man (Rep., 1952)
Trouble Along the Way (WB, 1953)
Island in the Sky (WB, 1953)
Hondo (WB, 1953)
The High and the Mighty (WB, 1954)
The Sea Chase (WB, 1955)

Blood Alley (WB, 1955)
The Conqueror (RKO, 1956)
The Searchers (WB, 1956)
Wings of Eagles (MGM, 1957)
Jet Pilot (Univ., 1957)
Legend of the Lost (UA, 1957)
The Barbarian and the Geisha (20th, 1958)
Rio Bravo (WB, 1959)
The Horse Soldiers (UA, 1959)
North to Alaska (20th, 1960)
The Alamo (UA, 1960)
The Comancheros (20th, 1961)
The Man Who Shot Liberty Valance (Par., 1962)
Hatari (Par., 1962)
The Longest Day (20th, 1962)
How the West Was Won (MGM, 1963)
Donovan's Reef (Par., 1963)
McLintock! (UA, 1963)
Circus World (UA, 1964)
The Greatest Story Ever Told (UA, 1965)
In Harm's Way (Par., 1965)
The Sons of Katie Elder (Par., 1965)
Cast a Giant Shadow (UA, 1966)
El Dorado (Par., 1967)
The War Wagon (Univ., 1967)
The Green Berets (WB-7 Arts, 1968)
Hellfighters (Univ., 1968)
True Grit (Par., 1969)
Undefeated (20th, 1969)
Chisum (WB-7 Arts, 1970)
Rio Lobo (NGP, 1970)
Big Jake (NGP, 1971)
Cowboys (WB-7 Arts, 1972)
Train Robbers (WB, 1973)
Cahill, U.S. Marshall (WB, 1973)
Mr. Q (WB, 1974)
Brannigan (UA, 1975)
Rooster Cogburn (Univ., 1975)
The Shootist (Par., 1976)

Clifton Webb
(1891–1966)

Clifton Webb began his theatrical career as a child actor. He studied art under Robert Henni with the ambition of becoming a painter. He also studied singing with Victor Maurel and made his opera debut with the Boston Opera Company. Returning to New York, he appeared in the Broadway musical hit *Love O'Mike* as a dancer with Peggy Wood. Success came next behind the footlights in London and Paris. He returned to Broadway to star opposite Marilyn Miller, Beatrice Lillie, Tamara Geva and Libby Holman in hit musicals. For a year and a half he toured in the national company of *The Man*

Clifton Webb

Who Came to Dinner. After a successful road tour he returned to Broadway in his greatest hit, Noel Coward's *Blith Spirit* which ran three seasons.

His first film appearance was in *Laura* (1944), directed by Otto Preminger. For that role he was nominated for an Oscar as best supporting actor. In 1946 he was nominated for his performance in *The Razor's Edge* and lost again. His last film under exclusive contract to 20th Century–Fox was *Satan Never Sleeps* with William Holden, released in 1962.

Clifton Webb Film Credits (1944–1962)

Laura (20th, 1944)	*The Razor's Edge* (20th, 1946)
The Dark Corner (20th, 1946)	*Sitting Pretty* (20th, 1946)

Ginger Rogers hosts a television show featuring old films of herself and co-star Clifton Webb *(right);* he seeks to stop the films from being shown as Fred Clark acts as the mediator, in *Dreamboat* (20th Century–Fox, 1952).

Mr. Belvedere Goes to College (20th, 1949)

Cheaper by the Dozen (20th, 1950)

For Heaven's Sake (20th, 1950)

Mr. Belvedere Rings the Bell (20th, 1951)

Elopement (20th, 1951)

Dreamboat (20th, 1952)

Stars and Stripes Forever (20th, 1952)

Titanic (20th, 1953)

Mister Scoutmaster (20th, 1953)

Woman's World (20th, 1954)

Three Coins in the Fountain (20th, 1954)

The Man Who Never Was (20th, 1956)

Boy on a Dolphin (20th, 1957)

The Remarkable Mr. Pennypacker (20th, 1959)

Holiday for Lovers (20th, 1959)

Satan Never Sleeps (20th, 1962)

Mae West
(1893–1980)

Mae West is a cattle baroness who inherits an oil field and becomes the wealthiest woman in the state. She yearns to become a lady in *Goin' to Town* with Luis Alberni (Paramount, 1935).

Mae West was born in Brooklyn, New York. At the age of seven she was winning prizes for her singing and tap dancing. She appeared in burlesque and then teamed up in a vaudeville act with Frank Wallace, whom she secretly married. The act broke up and that ended the marriage. Her first Broadway appearance was in 1911 in a Ned Wayburn revue, followed by *Vera Violetta*, which made her a Broadway name. She returned to vaudeville in 1915 as a star and began to write her own material. In 1926 she opened in her own play, *Sex*. The newspapers refused to advertise it and after 375 performances it was closed under public pressure. In the next two years she wrote and starred in two more plays. Her greatest success was in her play *Diamond Lil* which she took on tour. She went to Hollywood for a featured part in *Night After*

As the star of Alan Dinehart's Broadway show, Mae West complains to him that his musical could ruin her career in *The Heat's On* (Columbia, 1943).

Night with George Raft and stole the film. Her next film, opposite Cary Grant, was *She Done Him Wrong*. She made six more films at Paramount and was one of its highest paid stars. The Royal Air Force began calling its life jackets *Mae Wests* and so in 1940 her name was put in the dictionary. That same year she co-starred with W.C. Fields in the classic comedy *My Little Chickadee*. She returned to the theatre with great success in *Catherine Was Great*. She then revived *Diamond Lil* on Broadway and with it toured the United States and Great Britain. In later years she wrote books and plays and did nightclub work, record albums and an occasional film. She died at the age of 87, a Hollywood legend.

Mae West Feature Films (1932–1977)

Night After Night (Par., 1932)   1933)
She Done Him Wrong (Par.,   *I'm No Angel* (Par., 1933)

Belle of the Ninetire (Par., 1934)
Goin' to Town (Par., 1935)
Klondike Annie (Par., 1936)
Go West, Young Man (Par., 1936)
Every Day's a Holiday (Par., 1938)

My Little Chickadee (Univ., 1940)
The Heat's On (Col., 1943)
Myra Breckenridge (20th, 1970)
Sextette (Crown International Pictures, 1977)

Warren William
(1895–1948)

Warren William was born in Aitkin, Minnesota. His father was a newspaper publisher and as a youth he worked as a reporter. After serving in World War I he decided on a stage career and attended the American Academy of Dramatic Arts. Upon completion of his training there he acted in stock under his real name, Warren Krech. He appeared in a few silent films and played opposite Pearl White in the serial *Plunder*. Leading roles on Broadway in the middle twenties were followed by a contract with Warner Brothers in the early thirties when he appeared in numerous grade B films. Two prize roles came his way when he was cast by leading directors in *Lady for a Day* (Frank Capra) and as Ceasar in *Cleopatra*

Warren William

(Cecil B. DeMille). In the following years he played opposite Bette Davis, Claudette Colbert, Ruby Keeler, Kay Francis, Jean Arthur, Loretta Young and Mae West. In mystery films he played Philo Vance, Perry Mason and *The Lone Wolf* series.

Warren William *(right)*, playing the Lone Wolf for the fourth time in this successful series, is helped by Eric Blore in *The Lone Wolf Takes a Chance* (Columbia, 1941).

Warren William Sound Films (1931–1947)

Expensive Women (WB, 1931)
Honor of the Family (WB, 1931)
Women from Monte Carlo (WB, 1932)
Under Eighteen (WB, 1932)
The Mouthpiece (WB, 1932)
Beauty and the Boss (WB, 1932)
Dark Horse (WB, 1932)
Skyscraper Souls (WB, 1932)
Three on a Match (WB, 1932)
The Match King (WB, 1932)
Employees' Entrance (WB, 1933)
Mind Reader (WB, 1933)
Gold Diggers of 1933 (WB, 1933)
Lady for a Day (Col., 1933)
Goodbye Again (WB, 1933)
Bedside (WB, 1934)
Smarty (WB, 1934)
Dr. Monica (WB, 1934)
Upper World (WB, 1934)
Dragon Murder Case (WB, 1934)
Cleopatra (Par., 1934)
Case of the Howling Dog (WB, 1934)
Imitation of Life (Univ., 1934)
Outcast (Par., 1937)
Midnight Madonna (Par., 1937)
The Firefly (MGM, 1937)

Madame X (MGM, 1937)

Arsene Lupin Returns (MGM, 1938)

The First Hundred Years (MGM, 1938)

Wives Under Suspicion (Univ., 1938)

The Lone Wolf Spy Hunt (Col., 1939)

Gracie Allen Murder Case (Par., 1939)

The Man in the Iron Mask (UA, 1939)

Daytime Wife (20th, 1939)

The Lone Wolf Strikes (Col., 1940)

Lillian Russell (20th, 1940)

The Lone Wolf Meets a Lady (Col., 1940)

Arizona (Col., 1940)

Trail of the Vigilantes (Univ., 1940)

The Lone Wolf Takes a Chance (Col., 1941)

The Lone Wolf Keeps a Date (Col., 1941)

Wild Geese Calling (20th, 1941)

The Wolf Man (Univ., 1941)

One Dangerous Night (Col., 1943)

Passport to Suez (Col., 1943)

Strange Illusion (PRC, 1945)

Fear (Mon., 1946)

The Private Affairs of Bel Ami (UA, 1947)

Index

219

141740